CRIMINAL
INVESTIGATIONS

WHITE-COLLAR CRIME

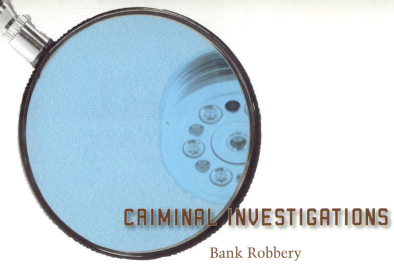

CRIMINAL INVESTIGATIONS

CRIMINAL INVESTIGATIONS

WHITE-COLLAR CRIME

MICHAEL BENSON

CONSULTING EDITOR: **JOHN L. FRENCH,**

CRIME SCENE SUPERVISOR,
BALTIMORE POLICE CRIME LABORATORY

CHELSEA HOUSE
PUBLISHERS

An imprint of Infobase Publishing

CRIMINAL INVESTIGATIONS: White-Collar Crime

Chelsea House
An imprint of Infobase Publishing
132 West 31st Street
New York NY 10001

Library of Congress Cataloging-in-Publication Data
Benson, Michael.
White-collar crime / Michael Benson ; consulting editor, John L. French.
p. cm. — (Criminal investigations)
Includes bibliographical references and index.
ISBN-13: 978-0-7910-9413-6 (alk. paper)
ISBN-10: 0-7910-9413-8 (alk. paper)
1. White collar crimes—United States—Case studies. 2. Commercial
crimes—United States. I. French, John L. II. Title. III. Series.
HV6769.B46 2008   364.16′80973—dc22
2008015642

Text design by Erika K. Arroyo
Cover design by Ben Peterson

Cover: Former Enron chairman Kenneth Lay leaves
the Bob Casey U.S. Courthouse after his fraud and conspiracy trial
on May 25, 2006, in Houston.

Printed in the United States of America

Bang EJB 10 9 8 7 6 5 4 3 2 1

This book is printed on acid-free paper.

All links and Web addresses were checked and verified to be
correct at the time of publication. Because of the dynamic nature
of the Web, some addresses and links may have changed
since publication and may no longer be valid.

To my Mom, Rita Alice Gertrude Treu Benson.

✦

Contents

Foreword

In 2000 there were 15,000 murders in the United States. During that same year about a half million people were assaulted, 1.1 million cars were stolen, 400,000 robberies took place, and more than 2 million homes and businesses were broken into. All told, in the last year of the twentieth century, there were more than 11 million crimes committed in this country.*

In 2000 the population of the United States was approximately 280 million people. If each of the above crimes happened to a separate person, only 4 percent of the country would have been directly affected. Yet everyone is in some way affected by crime. Taxes pay patrolmen, detectives, and scientists to investigate it, lawyers and judges to prosecute it, and correctional officers to watch over those convicted of committing it. Crimes against businesses cause prices to rise as their owners pass on the cost of theft and security measures installed to prevent future losses. Tourism in cities, and the money it brings in, may rise and fall in part due to stories about crime in their streets. And every time someone is shot, stabbed, beaten, or assaulted, or when someone is jailed for having committed such a crime, not only they suffer but so may their friends, family, and loved ones. Crime affects everyone.

It is the job of the police to investigate crime with the purpose of putting the bad guys in jail and keeping them there, hoping thereby to punish past crimes and discourage new ones. To accomplish this a police officer has to be many things: dedicated, brave, smart, honest, and imaginative. Luck helps, but it's not required. And there's one more virtue that should be associated with law enforcement. A good police officer is patient.

Patience is a virtue in crime fighting because police officers and detectives know something that most criminals don't. It's not a secret, but most lawbreakers don't learn it until it is too late. Criminals who make money robbing people, breaking into houses, or stealing cars; who live by dealing drugs or committing murder; who spend their days on the wrong side of the law, or commit any other crimes, must remember this: a criminal has to get away with every crime he or she commits. However, to get criminals off the street and put them behind bars, the police only have to catch a criminal once.

The methods by which police catch criminals are varied. Some are as old as recorded history and others are so new that they have yet to be tested in court. One of the first stories in the Bible is of murder, when Cain killed his brother Abel (Genesis 4:1–16). With few suspects to consider and an omniscient detective, this was an easy crime to solve. However, much later in that same work, a young man named Daniel steps in when a woman is accused of an immoral act by two elders (Daniel 13:1–63). By using the standard police practice of separating the witnesses before questioning them, he is able to arrive at the truth of the matter.

From the time of the Bible to almost present day, police investigations did not progress much further than questioning witnesses and searching the crime scene for obvious clues as to a criminal's identity. It was not until the late 1800s that science began to be employed. In 1879 the French began to use physical measurements and later photography to identify repeat offenders. In the same year a Scottish missionary in Japan used a handprint found on a wall to exonerate a man accused of theft. In 1892 a bloody fingerprint led Argentine police to charge and convict a mother of killing her children, and by 1905 Scotland Yard had convicted several criminals thanks to this new science.

Progress continued. By the 1920s scientists were using blood analysis to determine if recovered stains were from the victim or suspect, and the new field of firearms examination helped link bullets to the guns that fired them.

Nowadays, things are even harder on criminals, when by leaving behind a speck of blood, dropping a sweat-stained hat, or even taking a sip from a can of soda, they can give the police everything they need to identify and arrest them.

In the first decade of the twenty-first century the main tools used by the police include

- questioning witnesses and suspects
- searching the crime scene for physical evidence
- employing informants and undercover agents
- investigating the whereabouts of previous offenders when a crime they've been known to commit has occurred
- using computer databases to match evidence found on one crime scene to that found on others or to previously arrested suspects
- sharing information with other law enforcement agencies via the Internet
- using modern communications to keep the public informed and enlist their aid in ongoing investigations

But just as they have many different tools with which to solve crime, so too do they have many different kinds of crime and criminals to investigate. There is murder, kidnapping, and bank robbery. There are financial crimes committed by con men who gain their victim's trust or computer experts who hack into computers. There are criminals who have formed themselves into gangs and those who are organized into national syndicates. And there are those who would kill as many people as possible, either for the thrill of taking a human life or in the horribly misguided belief that it will advance their cause.

The Criminal Investigations series looks at all of the above and more. Each book in the series takes one type of crime and gives the reader an overview of the history of the crime, the methods and motives behind it, the people who have committed it, and the means by which these people are caught and punished. In this series celebrity crimes will be discussed and exposed. Mysteries that have yet to be solved will be presented. Readers will discover the truth about murderers, serial killers, and bank robbers whose stories have become myths and legends. These books will explain how criminals can separate a person from his hard-earned cash, how they prey on the weak and helpless, what is being done to stop them, and what one can do to help prevent becoming a victim.

John L. French,
Crime Scene Supervisor,
Baltimore Police Crime Laboratory

* Federal Bureau of Investigation. "Uniform Crime Reports, Crime in the United States 2000." Available online. URL: http://www.fbi.gov/ucr/ 00cius.htm. Accessed January 11, 2008.

Introduction:
"In the Course of His Occupation"

According to the Cornell University Law School, it was Edwin Sutherland—in a speech he gave to the American Sociological Society in 1939—who first used the phrase "white-collar crime." Sutherland told the group that the white-collar variety was "crime committed by a person of respectability and high social status in the course of his occupation."[1]

Although definitions and expert lists of what is and what isn't a white-collar crime vary, all white-collar crimes have three things in common:

1. They are nonviolent.
2. They take place in a commercial setting.
3. They are for profit.

White-collar crimes are all about money. No one gets physically hurt. As a rule, no one is even threatened. These crimes involve crooked business methods. They punch holes in the financial pipelines through which our money flows, and siphon off the leakage. White-collar crimes involve people from the business world who cheat to make money. Such criminals commit a wide variety of fraud.

Lying is normally not a crime. People fib frequently without breaking the law. There are limitations to this freedom, however.

For example, we are not allowed to lie in order to hurt someone else. This is called *slander*. We are not allowed to lie while under oath in a court of law. This is called *perjury*. And we are not allowed to lie in order to make money. That is called *fraud*. Fraud, in its broadest definition, would encompass all white-collar crime.

Fraud comes in all forms but always involves lying or deceiving in some manner to acquire greater sums of money than one would have honestly been owed. Wherever there is money, a smart crook has devised a theoretically foolproof way to rip it off. And, in many cases, the crook wears a suit, a tie, and a white shirt with a white collar while doing it.

White-collar crimes can involve credit cards, computers and the Internet, health care, insurance, mail, government, tax, and investment banking. There are business people illegally seeking monopolies, giving and getting kickbacks, counterfeiting, and stealing identities. There are elected officials who take bribes, embezzlers who steal money from the companies they run or work for, and corporate spies who steal secrets from their competitors.[2]

White-collar crime is expensive. According to the Federal Bureau of Investigation (FBI), illegal business practices cost the United States more than $300 billion every year. Much of that comes from the most common form of white-collar crime: cheating on tax returns.

Although white-collar crime is as old as history itself, it has— just like everything else—grown increasingly complex over time. The FBI says, "Today's con artists are more savvy and sophisticated than ever, engineering everything from slick online scams to complex stock and healthcare frauds."[3]

In this book we examine how white-collar criminals operate. We define how each scam works, and what law enforcement is doing to stop it. Of course, police and government agents attempt to catch and punish those who perpetrate these crimes. But just as much effort is put into educating people so that they are less vulnerable to white-collar criminals, who operate without conscience. Even the tragic events of September 11, 2001, have been exploited to commit white-collar crimes.

The book will begin with a brief overview of the history of white-collar crime. From there we take a look at the types of white-collar crime that most hurt our economy. We learn about the organizations that fight white-collar crime and the methods they use. Then we take a close-up look at the major types of white-collar crimes, focusing on the cases that have been broken by law enforcement, the cases in which the perps have been caught and punished. We look at corporate crime in which executives fleece their own investors. We look at consumer crimes, companies that use deception to sell something that, for one reason or another, isn't what it appears to be. Next up are crimes against the environment, committed by companies that cut corners to save money, and in the process foul the earth, the air, and the water. We then turn to the topic of insider trading, people who use their inside knowledge of a company's business to manipulate and profit from the trading of that company's stock.

White-collar crime changes with the times, so we'll also look at the most current type: computer crimes and identity theft—and the way officials are working to keep the Internet free of crooked practices. Finally, we'll examine the way money from several United States banks mysteriously emptied into the pockets of a few billionaires, the largest white-collar crime ever.

Businesspeople who are strong on smarts but weak on scruples will continue to invent new ways to break the rules and pad their bank accounts. Law enforcement, the judiciary system, and lawmakers must work together continuously to keep our criminal detection systems up to date.

Even though white-collar crimes are nonviolent, there is still a cost to society. White-collar crime hurts the average person. In some cases, taxpayers have to pay for losses caused by white-collar crimes. When corporations are destroyed by criminals, many people lose their jobs, and with them their health coverage and other benefits.

White-collar crime is nonviolent, but it can be vicious. The white-collar criminal is never going to walk up to a victim and punch him in the nose to rob him. This type of criminal does not wield a knife or a gun. But the millions of dollars he or she steals is the financial equivalent of thousands of armed robberies.

For example, when a manufacturer sells a product that he knows hurts people, maybe even kills people, but lies about the product's safety, isn't that violent? What about the sale of ineffective medicines to sick and desperate people? When those patients die, is that not violent?

Those who operate factories that foul the water and air, making everyone just a little bit sicker, are perpetrators of violent crimes—crimes against everyone's joy of life.

We rely on our government and law enforcement agencies to control our corporations. Yet American government on every level has been proven in some cases to be corrupt. On occasion, our elected officials and our white-collar criminals have proven to be one and the same.

Law enforcement handles white-collar crimes differently than other crimes, from the investigation to prosecution to incarceration. Cases brought against white-collar criminals are often not criminal cases at all, but rather civil suits. That is, victims sue the criminal to get their money back—plus some more as punishment. Even when criminal charges are brought against the corporate criminal, congressional subcommittees, rather than the local police department, conduct investigations.

The results are also clearly different when the criminal is convicted and sentenced to prison. The man who robbed the liquor store will be sent to a hell-on-earth penitentiary, while the white-collar criminal will be sent to a much nicer place for his jail-time. These low-security prisons are sometimes referred to as "country-club prisons," where the white-collar criminal is not punished as harshly as thieves who have stolen much less, but did it in a less sophisticated way.

Our investigation of white-collar crime starts with a quick history lesson to demonstrate how much—and how little—white-collar crime has changed over the years.

History of White-Collar Crime

Professor Edwin Sutherland defined white-collar crime as successful men with desk jobs stealing through the framework of their job. Although white-collar crime has always been around, it didn't become a major problem until the twentieth century, when corporations first became a major economic force.[1]

EARLY DAYS OF WHITE-COLLAR CRIME

In that same speech, Sutherland said that white-collar crime was a bigger problem than it appeared to be in the early twentieth century. White-collar criminals were not arrested by beat cops. If they got in trouble at all, white-collar criminals were punished by "administrative commissions" and civil rather than criminal courts.

White-collar criminals didn't go to jail in Sutherland's day. When punished at all, they paid a fine. As big companies became a larger piece of America's economic pie, corporate misconduct became more common. In the early twentieth century Upton Sinclair and other writers called *muckrakers* wrote articles and books about the injustices of corrupt and greedy corporate leaders.

THE GREAT DEPRESSION AND THE RISE OF MONOPOLIES

The point was driven home after the stock market crashed and the Great Depression began in 1929. The collapse of the stock market was caused in large part by corruption and unchecked greed.

During the Depression, everyone suffered. In 1933, with a large portion of the American public out of work and standing in soup lines to eat, an unnamed reporter for *The Nation* wrote, "If you steal $25, you're a thief. If you steal $250,000, you're an embezzler. If you steal $2,500,000, you're a financier."[2]

Writers also attacked monopolies. A monopoly is a business that operates without outside competition from other companies. Because they have the market to themselves, they can charge as much as they like for the product or service they are selling. In many cases those companies had unfairly wiped out the competition.

During the first decade of the twentieth century, huge companies bought up smaller companies to put them out of business, and the American dream of starting your own business became much more difficult to realize.

Monopolies also included groups of companies in the same business that agreed not to compete, so they could charge more for the product. The most famous monopoly, and the one that received the most attention, was Standard Oil, owned by John D. Rockefeller.

At the time people did not heed Sutherland's message. Between the end of World War II in 1945 and approximately 1970, America went through a period marked by a high degree of trust in large corporations. People believed that through the development of huge corporations, America would be richer and better than ever before. During this time corporate swindles continued.

FAMOUS WHITE-COLLAR SWINDLES

One of the most famous corporate swindles, known as the Great Salad Oil Swindle, happened in 1963. In this case the Allied Crude Vegetable Oil Refining Corporation used the simple scientific fact that oil floated atop water to create a great deception. The company sold shares in a stock of oil that didn't exist. Instead, they filled large casks with water and covered the top of each cask with a thin layer of oil. To anyone looking at the open cask, it appeared as if it were full of oil. Potential investors were then shown the open casks, saw all that oil, and invested their money. It wasn't until $175 million had been invested that the company was caught and the deception unearthed.[3] In December 1963 the architect of the swindle, Tino DeAngelis, was indicted on federal charges that he crossed state lines while carrying his ill-gained money.[4] DeAngelis was convicted in 1965 and served 10 years in prison.[5]

Another famous white-collar criminal of that era was Billy Sol Estes, who was a friend of Lyndon Baines Johnson, the vice-president under John F. Kennedy at the time. Estes charged ridiculously low prices for his product (fertilizer) and drove his competitors out of business. He supported his business by taking out huge loans, never failing to mention to the lenders that he was a friend of Vice President Johnson and that, as collateral, he was storing billions of dollars worth of grain in tanks on behalf of the United States government. In the salad oil case the tanks were real but the contents were phony. In this case, Estes was caught when it turned out the tanks full of grain did not exist. He was charged with fraud and convicted in 1963. He was sentenced to 15 years in prison but was released after eight.[6]

During the late 1960s and '70s changing social views made it increasingly fashionable to question authority. An unpopular war in

♀ GOULD AND FISK

In 1869 Jay Gould and Jim Fisk attempted to corner the gold market, that is, to eliminate all competitors. Unfortunately, what they did was mostly not illegal back then. However, it did lead to changes in the law.

Fisk and Gould wanted to buy up as much gold as they could—using other people's money, of course—and create a gold shortage. This would drive the price of gold way up, at which time they would sell their gold and make a fortune.

In the meantime, U.S. President Ulysses S. Grant planned to strengthen the nation's economy by reducing the amount of paper money (currency) in circulation. He planned to do this by buying up all of the currency and replacing it with dollar bills that were the equivalent of one dollar's worth of gold.

For Fisk and Gould to be successful they had to make sure that Grant did not carry out his plan to sell the nation's gold. To do this they hired a man named Abel Corbin to befriend Grant and

(continues)

(continued)

argue against the sale of gold. Corbin got as far as getting Grant to appoint General Daniel Butterfield, a man who had been bribed by Fisk and Gould, as assistant treasurer of the United States. But that was as far as the scheme went. Grant eventually caught on and sold the gold anyway. The sale caused the price of gold to fall, wiping out Fisk and Gould's many investors. The day this occurred—September 24, 1869—became known as Black Friday.

The scandal did not hurt Gould, who went on to own the Union Pacific Railroad. Fisk's luck wasn't as good. He was shot to death in 1872 by a jealous romantic rival.[7]

This 1885 cartoon depicts Jay Gould's almost complete control over the New York courts. Unlike Jim Fisk, Gould was able to attain great wealth and influence after their attempt to corner the gold market. *Bettmann/Corbis*

Vietnam, the Watergate scandal that led to President Nixon resigning from office in 1974, and political assassinations caused a large part of the public to question who had power and why. Because of this, the public looked at large corporations with greater scrutiny and skepticism.[8] During the 1970s law enforcement upped its efforts against the corruption of power, and several high-ranking officials were either indicted or forced to resign. Most notable among these was Vice President Spiro Agnew, who was forced to resign after being charged with not paying his taxes.[9]

TOUGH QUESTIONS AND PUBLIC ATTITUDES

By the end of the 1970s, the public was asking tough questions, such as why white-collar criminals received lighter sentences than their blue-collar counterparts. Were white-collar criminals treated better through every step of the justice system? And did criminal fraud go unhindered in the stock market, and in the sales of cars, liquor, and prescription drugs? The answer to all of these questions was *yes*, because the public, to date, was simply not well informed about nor outraged by white-collar crime. Very few wrote to their congressperson and asked that the government crackdown on white-collar crime. People worried about violent, personal crimes, such as getting mugged on the street or someone breaking into their home. They were not worried about crooked corporate executives or their impact on their lives.

One 1979 poll for a periodical called *Criminology* showed that white-collar crime, accounting for billions of stolen dollars, was ranked as less of a problem than street crime involving a theft larger than $25. One reason for this is that it can be difficult to understand the true impact of white-collar crime. Even when it is explained, the specialized financial practices and laws involved sometimes can put white-collar crime beyond the scope of the average person's understanding.[10]

Increasing public awareness didn't cut down on white-collar crime. In fact, the number of white-collar crimes skyrocketed in the 1980s, which became known as the "greed decade." In 1983 the FBI investigated almost 2,000 white-collar crimes, each involving greater than $100,000 in stolen money. By 1988 the number rose to 3,500.

WHITE-COLLAR CRIMINAL SUPERSTARS

The 1980s gave birth to white-collar criminal superstars. There was Ivan Boesky, who sold stock just before bad news about the stock was released. When the public heard the bad news, the price of the stock went down and Boesky re-bought it at the lower price, getting more stock for the same price. Knowing ahead of time that a stock's price will go up or down, and then using that information for personal gain, is called *insider trading*, and it is illegal. Before Ivan Boesky, who was sent to prison in 1987, practically no one had heard of insider training. After Boesky, many were familiar with the term.

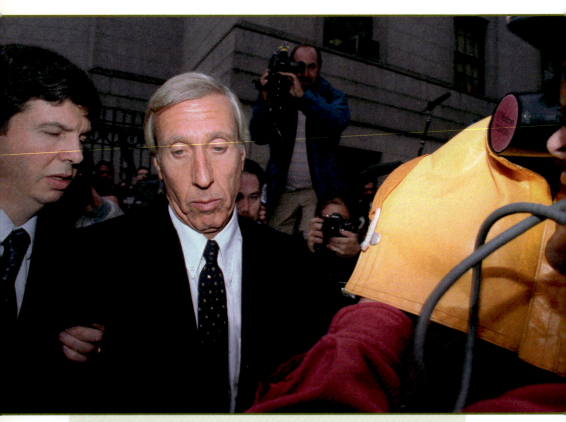

Members of the media surround corrupt financier Ivan Boesky and his attorney as they arrive at federal court in New York City, where he pleaded guilty to a criminal charge stemming from his insider trading. *Bettmann/Corbis*

Another white-collar criminal superstar of the 1980s was Michael Milken, who also used the stock market to make billions of dollars. He sold worthless stock for large sums to private citizens, banks, and insurance companies. The government at first attempted to investigate Milken's criminal dealings in 1987 through use of an informant, a man who would secretly tape record his conversations with Milken. In this case, the informant was another white-collar criminal named Ivan Boesky who agreed to spy on Milken in exchange for a shorter jail term. Boesky was not successful, however. Milken got wind of the trouble Boesky was in and refused to discuss his own operations with him. Federal investigators finally broke the Milken case in 1988 when Milken's top salesman agreed to cooperate with the investigation in exchange for immunity—that is, the government agreed not to prosecute the salesman because he was helping them gather evidence against a "bigger fish." In 1990 Milken was convicted, forced to pay a hefty fine of $600 million, and sentenced to 10 years in prison. That sentence, however, was later shortened to two years. When he was released from prison in 1993 he got a job as a business teacher at the University of California at Los Angeles (UCLA). Ironically, his students were not allowed to cheat.[11]

One of the largest white-collar crimes and largest thefts in history is the Savings and Loan scandal, which made headlines during the 1980s. The crimes ended up costing American taxpayers billions of dollars when the government was forced to spend huge sums to bail out failing banks. Estimates suggest that the amount of money stolen in all of the bank robberies in the twentieth century, when put together, would not have paid for one savings and loan buyout.[12]

Another famous case from the 1980s was that of Barry Minkow, the teenaged tycoon from Los Angeles who came close to making $80 million from a white-collar scam.

Minkow was a con artist who used trickery to steal money. Before Minkow tried his biggest scam, where he invented a company and convinced large corporations to invest in it, he tried a series of little scams that didn't work out that well. He called his company ZZZZ Best and claimed that it cleaned carpets.

He offered people free carpet cleanings. Once at the house with his equipment all set up, Minkow would find or fabricate a problem with the carpet or say that the carpet was too dirty to be cleaned with the simple free package they were giving away. Instead the carpet would need a more thorough job, one that would involve a charge. The customer, faced with a stranger in their home who had equipment already set up, usually agreed to pay for the service and Minkow would then vacuum. When he was done he would give the person a huge bill. He relied on his charm to get away with the scam and with the money.

Minkow liked to spend money as much as he liked to make it, and the vacuum scam was scrapped in favor of an insurance-fraud business. For example, in order to collect insurance money for damages, he kicked a hole in his own front door and claimed that an intruder did it.

There was also a list of stolen property that he wanted his insurance company to pay for, none of which had he ever owned. Finding that this scam wasn't worth his efforts, he came upon the idea of ripping off corporations in huge sums by pretending to be a tycoon. He made fake tax returns and financial statements and used these to convince powerful men that he was a rich man bound to get richer. At this time he was still a teenager, but he pretended to be older.

With all of that talent, one might wonder why Minkow didn't play by the rules. After all, he was clever enough to be a successful businessman. One theory is that the legitimate route to success might have been too slow for him. Or perhaps it was the art of the deception, the very fact that he was making his money by lying, by scamming, that made it so thrilling.

Minkow moved money around to conceal his deception, using money from new investors to pay old investors. After taking millions from corporate investors, Minkow offered ZZZZ Best stock to the public. He was becoming a star. He was worth millions of dollars, and the mayor of Los Angeles declared November 8, 1986, Barry Minkow Day.[13]

By this time, Minkow was famous in California and across the nation due to his many TV appearances. His company grew so large that it was able to take over several smaller carpet-cleaning companies. In 1987, at the age of 22, he was offered a partnership in the largest carpet-cleaning company in the United States, giving him a carpet-cleaning monopoly. This deal made him worth a whopping $650 million.

It was then that his balloon finally popped. On May 22, 1987, the *Los Angeles Times* published an investigative report that had looked into ZZZZ Best and had found that it was a *much* smaller operation than it pretended to be. The price of the company's stock plummeted. A few weeks later Minkow said that he was resigning as the chairman of ZZZZ Best because of poor health. The newspaper article sparked an investigation by law enforcement and Minkow was eventually arrested.

The young man was charged with

- bank, stock, and mail fraud, which involves lying to banks, selling bad stocks, and using the mail service to commit fraud
- money laundering, which is the practice of making stolen money look legitimate by passing it through legal businesses
- racketeering, or threatening people to make them pay money
- conspiracy, plotting with others to commit crimes
- tax evasion, hiding income to avoid paying taxes on it

ZZZZ Best, which had been considered a multimillion dollar carpet-cleaning powerhouse, was auctioned off, selling for a modest $62,000.

Minkow was charged with 57 white-collar crimes. He was tried in court and found guilty. The judge sentenced him to 25 years in prison. Minkow served five years and was released on parole in 1994.

During his time in prison he gave up being a carpet cleaner and became an evangelical preacher.[14] Is Minkow's new career sincere? According to one white-collar crime historian, "only God and Minkow know for sure."[15]

These days Minkow also works side-by-side with FBI agents to help find, arrest, and successfully prosecute white-collar criminals. His operation is called the Fraud Discovery Institute, and he investigates reports of white-collar crimes and turns his results over to federal agents. Among his successes are the 2005 arrest of a Long Island con man who was recruiting investors to put their money into a phony fund, and the 2007 arrest of a Brooklyn man who convinced the elderly into putting their money into imaginary property.[16]

WHITE-COLLAR CRIMINAL RESEARCH

During the last 80 years, the government has spent millions of dollars gathering statistics on violent crime and street crime. But comparatively little has been spent researching white-collar crime.

Wearing his prison jumpsuit for dramatic effect, convicted con artist Barry Minkow gives a sermon on materialism in a San Diego church. *Denis Poroy/AP*

One reason for this is that much white-collar crime is never reported or detected, making it almost impossible, for example, to say with any degree of accuracy how much money is sucked out of the economy every year by white-collar crime. If a white-collar criminal is clever, the victim may never know that he has been robbed. He might simply think that the problem was with his own decision making, bad luck, or timing regarding his investments.

One early method of rooting out corporate crime was to keep a list of all legal actions against major corporations, even if the infractions were small. The government believed that a company that breaks small rules might also tend to break big rules. One such survey of American corporations done in the 1940s showed that more than half of the corporations studied had been convicted repeatedly on criminal charges, not counting civil suits (victims suing the corporation in an attempt to get their money back).

Marshall Clinard and Peter Yeager conducted a similar study in the 1970s, and published the results in their book, *Corporate Crime*. They found that things had not gotten any better, and in fact, they'd gotten worse. Their study also revealed that 10 percent of the corporations studied accounted for more than half of the criminal violations cited. Large corporations were more apt to be crooked than smaller ones, and the most corruption was in the oil, prescription drug, and automotive industries.[17] The study revealed that "white-collar crime is relatively commonplace among large corporations."[18] And that was ignoring the fact that corporate crimes often went unreported.

White-collar crime again made the headlines in 1992 when investigative journalists revealed that the members of the U.S. House of Representatives were allowed to write checks against House bank accounts that seemingly had no limits. It is illegal to purposefully write checks for more funds than one has in a checking account, but in this case Congress was given a bottomless money pit. One of the most shocking things about the system, whereby members of Congress could bounce checks without being penalized in any way, was that the system had been in place since 1830. Still, the news of "Rubbergate," as the scandal was called, was such that in 1994 many congresspersons who might have expected to be easily re-elected found themselves voted out of office.[19]

Even in the face of this government scandal, public outrage was minimal. When a Wall Street investment firm known as Salomon Brothers was exposed in 1991 as having illegally cornered the treasury bond market (that is, they illegally eliminated their competitors) and had artificially inflated its profits, there was little outcry. According to *Profit Without Honor*, "There were no widespread cries to ban Salomon Brothers from the government securities market. Radio talk shows did not fill the airwaves with the voices of angry callers. Officers at big investment firms did not fear they would lose their jobs because of the public outcry." Despite the fact that the cost to American taxpayers might run into the billions of dollars because of changing interest rates caused by the Salomon Brothers' crimes, there was no public anger, and bonuses for brokerage executives that year were higher than ever.[20]

Types of
White-Collar Crime

Sondra is sitting at her computer answering e-mail. It appears that she's gotten a notice about her bank account so she clicks to open it. Sure enough, it looks just like the other e-mails she's received from her bank. The e-mail says, "We have discovered that there is a problem with your savings account. Before we can tell you more we have to make sure you are the holder of the account. Please fill out the following form." And the form asks for Sondra's birthday, social security number, and personal identification number (P.I.N.) that she uses to get cash out of an ATM. She fills in the form, click, and boom, the e-mail goes away and she's staring at her desktop.

Sondra has just become the victim of a white-collar crime. The e-mail was not from her bank at all. It was a fake, a counterfeit, cleverly designed to fool the recipient. It came from a thief who wanted to steal someone's identity, and now—armed with all of Sondra's personal information—the thief can quickly drain Sondra's account and ruin her credit. That's called computer fraud. In this chapter we are going to look at some of the more common types of white-collar crime and look at examples of each.

MONOPOLIES, TRUSTS, AND PRICE-FIXING

In big business, a trust happens when corporations get together to reduce competition and control prices. In a fair world, customers should have the choice of buying the best product for the lowest price, but when a trust occurs, they do not have that option. Even though several companies may be making the same product, the companies will make no effort to make their product better than the other's, and prices will rise and fall together. This is called price-fixing.

A group of companies that cooperate rather than compete are sometimes called *cartels*. If competition doesn't exist because one corporation has, in one way or another, wiped out the competition, this is called a *monopoly*. Whether it be because of a cartel or a monopoly, lack of competition is always bad for the consumer, who ends up paying more for less.

As far back as the nineteenth century, laws have been passed in the United States to control cartels and monopolies. The Sherman Act, passed in 1890, made all cartels and some monopolies illegal. The act, however, did not punish manufacturers who dominated a particular market simply because they were best able to create a product. For example, if everyone drank Coke instead of Pepsi because Coke tasted better, Coke would not be breaking the law. If Coke and Pepsi get together and agree to always raise the price of their product at the same time so consumers never have a cheaper option, then they are violating the Sherman Act.[1] Laws that promote fair competition are called anti-trust laws.

COMPUTER AND INTERNET FRAUD

Computer and Internet fraud crimes involve any unauthorized use of a computer. Crimes may include using the Internet to get a victim's credit card or social security number, spreading viruses through the Internet that will harm business, or using a computer to "hack" into and damage a company's computer system. This might be done, for example, by a competitor as an attempt to gain an unfair advantage in the market.

The FBI is limited in its ability to look at the public's private computer information by the same laws that prohibit law enforcement from entering your home on a whim and demanding to see your files. Before any law enforcement agency can look at a person's private records, whether those records are on paper or stored in a computer, the agency needs a search warrant.[2]

Computer scientists look at graphs from anti-fraud software developed for Internet auction sites like eBay. *Keith Srakocic/AP*

PHONE AND TELEMARKETING FRAUD

These are crimes in which the criminals use the telephone to contact potential victims. Catching these types of criminals can be difficult because they use fake names and transmit false numbers through the potential victim's caller ID system. These operations move from place to place, frequently change phone numbers, and often manage to stay one step ahead of the law.

In some cases these criminals call on the phone or send an e-mail asking for money for a charity. If a victim sends them money,

⚲ SEARCH WARRANTS

To search a building or computer, law enforcement officers need a search warrant. This legal document, signed by a judge, states what is being searched for and that the search is warranted, meaning evidence presented by police gives reasonable cause to believe a crime has been committed.[3]

UNITED STATES DISTRICT COURT
FOR THE DISTRICT OF COLUMBIA

In the Matter of the Search of
(Name, address or brief description of person or property to be searched)

RAYBURN HOUSE OFFICE BUILDING
ROOM NUMBER 2113
WASHINGTON, DC 20515

SEARCH WARRANT

CASE NUMBER: 06 - 2 3 1 M - 01.

TO: TIMOTHY R. THIBAULT and any Authorized Officer of the United States

Affidavit(s) having been made before me by DETECTIVE, TIMOTHY R. THIBAULT who has reason to believe
that ☐ on the person or ☒ on the premises known as (name, description and or location)

Rayburn House Office Building, Room Number 2113, Washington, DC 20515.
See Schedule A

in the District of Columbia, there is now concealed a certain person or property, namely (describe the person or property)

See Schedules A, B, C and the affidavit submitted in support of the application for this warrant which are incorporated
herein by reference.

I am satisfied that the affidavits(s) and any recorded testimony establish probable cause to believe that the person or
property so described is now concealed on the person or premises above-described and establish grounds for the issuance
of this warrant.

YOU ARE HEREBY COMMANDED to search on or before *May 21, 2006*
(Date)

(not to exceed 10 days) the person or place named above for the person or property specified, serving this warrant and
making the search ☐ (in the daytime - 6:00 A.M. to 10:00 P.M.) ☒ (at any time in the day or night as I find reasonable
cause has been established) and if the person or property be found there to seize same, leaving a copy of this warrant and
receipt for the person or property taken, and prepare a written inventory of the person or property seized and promptly
return this warrant to the undersigned U.S. Judge/U.S. Magistrate Judge, as required by law. *The US Capital*
police are directed to provide complete
access to the property described herein.

at Washington, D.C.

Date and Time Issued
HOGAN, C. J. Tr.

Name and Title of Judicial Officer   *Chief Judge*

Signature of Judicial Officer
5-18-06
5 pm

In 2006 FBI agents obtained a warrant to search the congressional offices of Louisiana Representative William Jefferson in the Rayburn House Office Building in Washington D.C. Jefferson was indicted on charges of bribery and other crimes in 2007. The case remains open as of this writing. *U.S. District Court/AP* however, it goes directly into the criminal's pocket rather than to the charity.

A recent scheme using both the phone and the computer involves jury duty. Criminals have been randomly contacting people and telling them that they have been chosen for jury duty. They then ask to verify the person's identity by asking for date of birth and social security number. The victim may not realize that they haven't actually been chosen for jury duty until they report to the courthouse as much as several weeks later, and by that time their identity has been stolen.

The key to protecting yourself from becoming a victim of phone and telemarketing fraud is to never give personal information or money to someone you don't know over the phone or through e-mail. There are several warning signs of fraud. If a caller or an e-mailer says the following things, it should raise a red flag of suspicion:

- "You must act now or the offer won't be good."
- "You've won a free gift, vacation, or prize." But you have to pay for "postage and handling" or other charges.
- "You must send money, give a credit card or bank account number, or have a check picked up by courier." You may hear this before you have had a chance to consider the offer carefully.
- "You don't need to check out the company with anyone." The callers say you do not need to speak to anyone including your family, lawyer, accountant, local Better Business Bureau, or consumer protection agency.
- "You don't need any written information about the company or references."
- "You can't afford to miss this 'high-profit, no-risk' offer."[4]

CREDIT CARD FRAUD

Credit card fraud involves any unauthorized use of a credit card to purchase merchandise or services. There are several ways a criminal can go about committing this crime.

The thief can do it the old-fashioned way and pick someone's pocket. Before the victim realizes his wallet is gone, the thief can buy thousands of dollars worth of merchandise.

A thief can, if he's talented, make a counterfeit credit card. Just as money counterfeiters design and print their own paper money, an artist who knows how to use a plastic press could create a phony card. This is much tougher to do than it once was. Today's credit cards are "swiped" and a computer reads tiny electronic coding on the card. The coding is next to impossible for a counterfeiter to reproduce. Also, many of today's credit cards have three-dimensional images on them, also difficult to copy.

With some transactions, such as those made over the phone or online, the credit card itself is not necessary to purchase merchandise. Only the card number is needed. A thief can steal a credit card

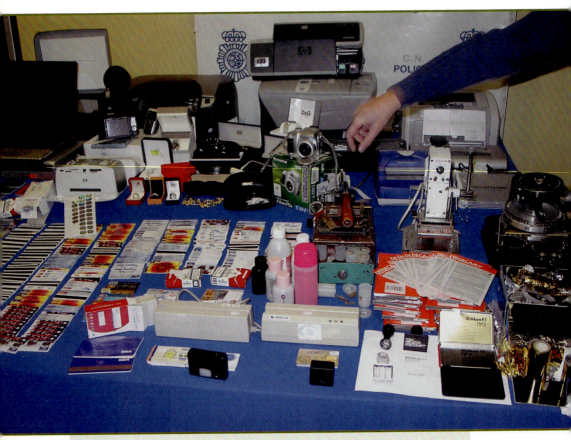

A policeman shows a display of fake credit cards and the equipment used to make them in Madrid in November 2006. *Spanish National Police/AP*

number by sending a fake e-mail asking for it. Some thieves even go through garbage looking for carbon copies of credit card transactions, just to steal the number.

Finally, a criminal could commit credit card fraud by obtaining a real credit card through false pretenses, that is, by pretending they are someone they aren't.

BANKRUPTCY FRAUD

The law allows those who are hopelessly in debt to be relieved of that debt by declaring bankruptcy, that is, an official promise not to borrow any more money for a set period of time. White-collar criminals can exploit these laws to get out of paying debts, then change their identity so that new loans can be secured.

HEALTH CARE FRAUD

Health care fraud occurs when people take advantage of health care providers, health insurance companies, or government health care programs, such as Medicaid and Medicare, to wrongfully gain money. The number-one type of health care fraud involves billing patterns. Doctors will perform a small task for a patient, such as treat them for a cold, but will bill the insurance company for something more serious, such as setting a broken leg. In some billing fraud cases, every bill sent from the fraudulent doctor's office to an insurance company was exaggerated in some way.

Other types of health care fraud include kickbacks (a sum of money paid illegally in exchange for favors), billing a premium rate for services performed by a person less qualified than the billing doctor, and billing for unnecessary equipment.

Law enforcement has found significant health care fraud going on at all types of health care facilities: hospitals, doctors' offices, ambulance services, laboratories, drug stores, medical equipment suppliers, and nursing homes.[5]

ENVIRONMENTAL CRIME

Some white-collar laws prohibit crimes against the planet, also called environmental crimes. For example, to increase profits, a corporate executive might order that his factory's toxic waste be disposed of through cheaper means than the law requires. Instead of being properly handled, that waste, whether it is poisonous or radioactive or both, might be dumped into a river. Because of the crime, a river is turned foul and the surrounding community is negatively affected.[6] Any unauthorized dumping of a toxic substance into the environment (air, water, or soil) that could harm people, property, or cause air or water pollution, is considered an environmental crime.[7]

In Chapter 6 we will take a detailed look at a small community called Love Canal in Upstate New York that was built on top of toxic landfill, with tragic consequences.

GOVERNMENTAL CRIME

These are crimes committed by elected officials, using their political power to pad their pockets with cash. It is not uncommon for public officials to pass laws and make rules that steer government money into their home community. Sometimes individuals are responsible and, as is true of corporate crime, sometimes the corruption gets inside the fabric of the system and becomes part of "how things operate."[8]

The Federal Bureau of Investigation

In movies or TV shows police sometimes swoop down upon a crime-ridden neighborhood, herd a group of criminals into a paddy wagon, and take them off to jail. The successful conclusion of FBI investigations into white-collar crime is sometimes just as dramatic. Take for example "Operation Continued Action." The operation, which focused on fraud against banks, involved 158 separate investigations among 47 field offices in 37 states, and targeted 271 suspects. When investigations had gathered enough evidence, more than 150 of those suspects were arrested at the same time. There might not have been a paddy wagon, but there was plenty of justice.[1]

The Federal Bureau of Investigation is the national police force of the United States. It investigates crimes that are spread out across several states, or across national borders—crimes that would be impossible for local or state police forces to tackle.

According to an FBI study, there was a 300 percent increase in white-collar crime in the United States between 2001 and 2005.[2] Most of that increase came from corporate crime and stock market scams. The criminals involved were successful businessmen. They were millionaires who wanted to become billionaires and were willing to break the law to do it. On a grand scale, they sold shares of a stock that seemed to have value but in reality did not.[3]

DR. JOHN ACKA BLAY-MIEZAH: THE "RICHEST MAN IN THE WORLD"

The CBS news magazine *60 Minutes* is known for exposing white-collar criminals. The most successful man *60 Minutes* ever exposed was Dr. John Acka Blay-Miezah, who claimed to be the richest man in the world. He claimed to be in sole possession of something called the Oman-Ghana fund.

In this scam, Blay-Miezah asked other people for money to supposedly free up the Oman-Ghana funds; he claimed he would eventually pay out 10 dollars for every dollar he received. Without giving much more detail than that, he had people waiting in line to invest in his fund.

In January 1989 *60 Minutes*, with Ed Bradley reporting, ran a piece on Blay-Miezah, saying that, despite the fact that he had accumulated close to a billion dollars using his story, he had yet to pay out a dime.

When Bradley interviewed the man in person, "he was living in luxury in London, thanks to the gullibility and greed of his American investors whom he'd bilked." Blay-Miezah died sometime in the late 1990s before authorities had an opportunity to recover any of the money he'd stolen.[4]

THE FBI ON WHITE-COLLAR CRIME

Today's FBI is well equipped, both with technology and personnel, to fight the growing white-collar crime problem. The FBI's stated goal is to "reduce the level of significant white-collar crime."[5]

In recent years the FBI has hired and trained special agents and analysts who are experts on how huge corporations work and how large-scale corporate crime works. Crime schemes are sometimes so complex and so hidden in the paperwork of a company that it takes a specially trained analyst to tell the difference between fraud and legitimate business.

Even then, FBI investigations into white-collar crime can be time-consuming and costly. To respond to the growth in corporate crime, the FBI has set the following priorities:

- increase the number of agents and analysts looking for suspicious activity in private corporations but also in "government regulators, and all levels of law enforcement"
- begin full-scale investigations when suspicious behavior is detected
- use power to take ill-gained money away from white-collar criminals
- better train future operatives so that complex investigations will take less time and cost less money[6]

According to FBI studies, the dollar that is most apt to be ripped off by white-collar crime is the tax dollar. This means that U.S. citizens are paying most of the bill for rich corporate criminals to get even richer.

INVESTIGATING HEALTH CARE FRAUD

Individual FBI agents and analysts specialize in different types of white-collar crime. For example, there is one group of agents who work only on cases of health care fraud. They investigate frauds involving both government-sponsored insurance programs, such as Medicare and Medicaid, as well as private-insurer programs. Because the health care industry is so complicated, the FBI relies on cooperation with other government agencies that deal with health care.

Health care fraud is high on the FBI's priority list because this crime holds unlimited potential for the criminal. For example, if a patient is insured by a private company, the other patients who use that company's insurance end up paying for the stolen money through higher insurance premiums. The FBI has learned that victims of health care fraud often make excellent volunteers for undercover FBI missions, seeing their doctor and then reporting back to the FBI exactly what services they received. This allows the bureau to compare that evidence with what the doctor charged for the visit. If there is a big difference between the two, they know they have found a doctor who may be using fraudulent billing practices to steal money from the insurance company.

FBI investigations show that the problem of health care fraud often goes beyond stealing done by individual doctors. The fraud is sometimes system-wide, spanning "national regional chains of service providers."[7] In those situations it is exceedingly difficult to see, from the outside, that improper billing practices are taking place. The patient is the only one who knows what treatment he or she received, but the patient is not in direct communication with the insurance company. The doctor's staff usually takes care of all the paperwork.

In order for the FBI to determine a crime has been committed, they need to hear from a patient who has been treated by a crooked health care provider and from the insurance company to whom the provider sent the bill. Only by comparing both sets of information can the FBI demonstrate that a crime has taken place.

In addition to simple cases in which doctors over-bill insurance companies for their services, there are also frauds involving billing for prescription drugs, the purchase of at-home medical equipment for the seriously ill, transportation services, and outpatient and home health care services.[8]

THE FBI ON CORPORATE CRIME

The FBI has also focused on financial institution fraud, such as trading stocks with insider information and identity theft. In order to best investigate corporate crimes, the FBI must stay on good terms with the corporations. The FBI's efforts to maintain good relations with corporations include not just the older, well-established corporations, but newer corporations as well. Any corporation can be struck by this type of crime. It just takes one bad employee robbed of his scruples by greed.

Along with being skilled at maintaining these relationships with corporations, the bureau's operatives are experts on how corporations work. They know the right questions to ask and are able to determine the truthfulness of the answers.

If the crimes are being committed against the corporation by outside forces, FBI operatives are trained to recognize any organization that might potentially be illegally draining a corporation's funds. Operatives look for these types of drains at the local, regional, national, or even global level. The FBI wants it known that it can and will "conduct worldwide investigations" if it means taking apart "criminal enterprises engaged in significant financial institution fraud."[9]

Sen. Susan Collins and U.S. Attorney Jay McCloskey, right, make phone calls to Maine residents as part of an effort to warn people who may be targets of fraudulent telemarketers. This tactic is also employed by the FBI when trying to prevent fraudulent telemarketing or telephone fraud. *Joel Page/AP*

There was a time when the best law enforcement could hope for was to catch, prosecute, convict, and fine a corporate criminal. Now FBI special agents get to see the criminal behind bars, and that provides the ultimate satisfaction.

New laws give the bureau another punishment option. Along with doing time, the criminal can be forced to give back the money stolen. Like drug dealers, white-collar criminals can often be caught through money-laundering operations, in which money changes hands under false pretenses to disguise the actual, illegal manner in which the money was acquired. The FBI is well trained in recognizing organizations that take part in this process or exist only to launder money.

Another form of white-collar crime the FBI has targeted is fraudulent telemarketing or telephone fraud. This is a fake sales pitch given over the phone in an attempt to get the customer to give up cash or a key identification number, such as a credit card or a social security number.

These crimes are not easily fought by local law enforcement because the phone calls are made long distance, across state lines. Local police are not allowed to investigate crimes that take place outside their territory or jurisdiction. The FBI, on the other hand, can investigate crimes committed anywhere in the United States, and, in many cases, in other nations as well. With telemarketing crime, sometimes the calls come from outside the United States. (This is also true of some forms of insurance fraud that cross jurisdictional lines and can only be effectively investigated by the FBI.)

Because telephone crimes can be limited if potential victims are warned about them ahead of time, the FBI has programs to educate the public. These programs focus on those most apt to be victimized, such as the elderly.

The FBI also keeps an eye out for environmental crimes. According to the FBI, "Because serious public health and safety concerns relate to environmental crime, the FBI will enhance its working relationships with federal, state, and local investigative and regulatory agencies to address this crime problem."[10]

Part of the FBI's battle against corporate crime is psychological. If criminals think they can get away with it, they'll try it, and some will succeed. If they don't think they can get away with it, they might not try.

The FBI wants everyone to know that they are keeping an eye out for unusual accounting numbers or practices that might indicate a white-collar crime, and that the punishments for committing a white-collar crime are harsher than ever.

The risk of getting caught for a white-collar crime is very high. Teams of FBI scientists and computer experts are working to create computer software that will make a lot of current white-collar crimes impossible or, at least, much more difficult to commit. For example, many investigative techniques devised to combat international terrorism in the days following September 11, 2001, have turned out to be effective against corporate crime since both international terror and white-collar crime involve the illegal funneling of money.

As the national law-enforcement agency, the FBI is responsible for those who are stealing federal government tax dollars, money that is supposed to go toward things like education, interstate highways, and defense. In order to better fight this type of crime, the FBI has "increased its intelligence base." That means that FBI eyes and ears are everywhere.

The FBI is not alone when it comes to the battle against white-collar crime. Other federal organizations, such as the Federal Trade Commission, also work to keep things on the up and up. Also fighting the good fight are

- the U.S. Department of the Treasury's Secret Service, which is in charge of anticounterfeiting efforts as well as of protecting the president of the United States
- the Office of Terrorism and Financial Intelligence (TFI)
- the Financial Crimes Enforcement Network (FinCEN)
- the Office of Intelligence and Analysis (OIA)
- the Office of Foreign Assets Control (OFAC)
- the Criminal Investigation (CI) branch of the Internal Revenue Service (IRS)
- the Department of Justice's Drug Enforcement Administration (DEA)
- the Asset Forfeiture Money Laundering Section (AFMLS) of the Department of Justice's Criminal Division
- the United States Postal Inspection Service (USPIS)[11]

An agent of the Office of Foreign Assets Control closes the door to a storage unit in Columbia, Missouri, in October 2004. Several computers, files, and a fax machine were confiscated in a terror financing investigation. *Don Shrubshell/AP*

Numbers show that the Federal Bureau of Investigation has taken a huge bite out of white-collar crime. Between 2000 and 2004, FBI white-collar crime investigations resulted in 11,500 convictions, resulting in $8.1 billion in fines. True, the FBI loves to punish criminals, but they also love the fact that these arrests will prevent possible future criminals from being tempted to commit white-collar crimes.[12]

ABSCAM:
How to Catch
White-Collar Criminals

One tried-and-true method of breaking up any type of organized crime, including the white-collar variety, is to use informants, undercover agents sometimes known as *moles*. Police investigating Mafia groups, for example, have used informants to help arrest mobsters and break up mobs. This same technique was used in a white-collar bust that made the front pages of the newspapers for days.

Some white-collar crimes are committed by elected officials. They have power, and the greater the power a person or corporation has, the more tempting it can become to make money by stealing it. The chances of getting caught seem slim, so it's often a matter between the elected official and his conscience.

In one famous case an undercover agent was used to bust up organized corruption among United States elected officials. It's the scandal that became known around the world as ABSCAM.

CON MAN TURNED INFORMANT

The informant's name was Melvin Weinberg, and his role was one of necessity rather than choice. Weinberg was a con man, a swindler, who had been convicted of fraud and was looking to cut a deal. He could either spy on elected officials suspected of corruption, or he could go to jail. In 1978 Weinberg chose to work with the FBI. Under the FBI's guidance, he set up a fake company called Abdul Enterprises, which was supposedly owned by an Arab sheik that didn't exist.

Weinberg let suspected corrupt politicians know that Sheik Abdul was a billionaire who wanted to take his money out of Arab banks and invest it in all things American. The politicians were told that the sheik was willing to bribe all of the necessary officials if

Mayor Angelo Errichetti, left, of Camden, NJ, and Rep. Raymond Lederer of Pennsylvania are shown as they appear at U.S. District Court in Brooklyn, NY, to answer indictments in the ABSCAM probe. *Bettmann/Corbis*

he could cut through the red tape that might ordinarily prevent or delay him from investing his money as he chose.

The first politician to fall into the trap was the mayor of Camden, New Jersey. Mayor Angelo Errichetti agreed to take a bribe in exchange for helping the sheik get a gambling license so the foreign billionaire could open a casino in Atlantic City. As an example of the small details—the little touches that make a con job work— Weinberg purchased a knife at a flea market and sent it to the Camden mayor, saying that it was a thank-you gift from the sheik, a rare tribal knife worth millions.

The mayor bragged to others about the gift. When Weinberg asked the mayor to have a private meeting with representatives of the sheik, the mayor eagerly agreed. The room where the meeting took place featured actors playing the sheik's representatives and was filmed and recorded by a hidden camera. The mayor was told that the sheik was having troubles in his homeland and wanted to come to the United States to live. The mayor said that he could make that easier for the sheik, but it was going to cost another $100,000. The final FBI film of the mayor showed him accepting this additional bribe. He was indicted in 1979, and eventually convicted of bribery, fined $40,000, and sentenced to six years in prison.[1]

New Jersey Representative Frank Thompson was caught in the same trap, agreeing to take $50,000 in exchange for helping with the sheik's immigration problems while the FBI watched and listened.

U.S. Senator Harrison Arlington Williams, Jr. also took the bait. He and his legal-firm partners agreed to take control of the sheik's investment strategy. They said that they wanted to "borrow" $100 million from the sheik to buy a titanium mine in Virginia, but the mine was not going to have any titanium and the sheik would never get his money back. The senator was caught red-handed when he told Weinberg that he knew how to channel tax dollars in the sheik's direction through government contracts. The senator did not know that the room was wired and the FBI was listening.

A USEFUL INVESTIGATION

The ABSCAM investigation lasted only about a year. By that time other elected officials were wise to the fact that something was up. Politicians became more cautious and avoided risky situations. Weinberg later said that he wished the investigation could have gone on longer, and estimated that a third of the nation's congresspersons would have been arrested had they all been told about the fake sheik and his troubles.

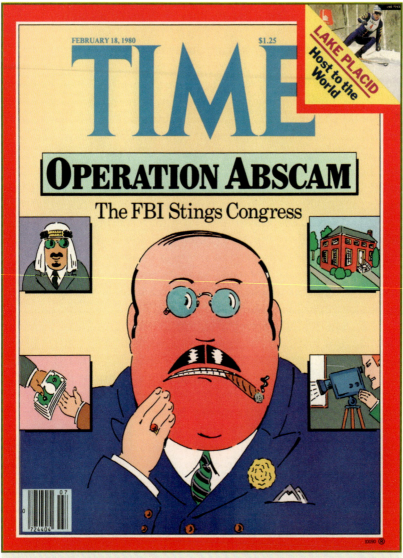

The February 18, 1980, *Time* cover on the ABSCAM investigation. *Time &
Life Pictures/Getty Images*

Along with learning that many elected officials were willing to take a bribe in exchange for a favor, ABSCAM also exposed the close relationship between some elected officials and members of organized crime. One of Senator Williams' partners in the titanium mine scam was a close associate of mob boss Meyer Lansky.

The most stunning visual captured by the FBI cameras was Representative Richard Kelly of Florida who, when presented with a suitcase full of money, began to cry about how poor he was as he shoved packets of money into his pants pockets. He later earned public scorn when, in his own defense at his trial, he said that he was only pretending to take the money as part of his one-man anti-corruption investigation. Nobody believed him.

Seven members of Congress were arrested and taken to trial. The common defense was that they were greedy but not corrupt, and that they saw taking money from the sheik as a way to make money doing nothing, and certainly that wasn't against the law.

One claimed that, yes, that was him on the film taking the bribe, but he was drunk at the time and didn't know what he was doing. The jury didn't buy it, however, and sentenced him to three years in prison.

♀ EDUCATING LAW ENFORCEMENT

One way to decrease the amount of white-collar crime is to better educate people—in particular law-enforcement personnel—as to how these crimes are best identified and halted. The FBI has programs whereby they teach other law-enforcement agencies, at any level, about white-collar crime.

One institution that is stepping up to educate future cops and lawyers about white-collar crime is Roberts Wesleyan College, just outside of Rochester, New York. The school introduced a new bachelor of science major in economic-crime investigation during the fall of 2006.[2]

According to Robert Hallman, director of criminal justice and sociology at Roberts Wesleyan, "While there are 17,000 local, state and federal police agencies across the country, there's little to no preparation to combat white-collar crime. Officers are trained to

(continues)

(continued)

deal with street crime, they're not trained to investigate identity theft, consumer fraud, and embezzlement."

The economic-crime investigation program has courses in criminal justice, accounting, and computer science. Students will specialize either in accounting or computers. The college is also creating courses on white-collar crime, computer forensics, and computer network security.

Graduates should be able to find work in either law enforcement or the private sector. The Wesleyan program is not the only education on white-collar crime available, even in the Western New York State area. There is also an associate's degree program at Genesee Community College and a bachelor's degree program at Hilbert College in Erie County.[3]

Amazingly, one of the congressmen, Raymond Lederer, was reelected after being involved in the ABSCAM scandal. A hearing to decide who would serve on his jury was taking place as he was sworn in to serve another term in office.[4]

Senator Williams went on trial in 1981, using the "greedy-not-corrupt" defense. His jury disagreed and he was sentenced to three years in prison. Williams became the first United States senator to be sent to prison since 1905.[5]

The ABSCAM investigation was very effective when it came to weeding out public officials who were corrupt, but it raised ethical issues. Law enforcement is not allowed to tempt people into committing crimes and then arrest them for doing so. That is called *entrapment*. To put it another way, police are supposed to catch criminals, not create them.

Some argued that was exactly what the FBI was doing with ABSCAM. The argument in favor of the investigation was that the subjects were limited to publicly elected officials who, because of their position, are expected to adhere to a moral code.[6]

Crimes Against Consumers

In one form of white-collar crime, the criminals are the stores people shop in and the clerks who sell you things. The victim, of course, is the consumer. The federal organization set up to combat this type of crime is the Federal Trade Commission (FTC), and it deals with a number of different criminal activities.

BAIT AND SWITCH

The FTC defines *bait and switch* as "an alluring but insincere offer to sell a product or service which the advertiser does not intend or want to sell."[1]

The FTC guideline prohibiting this type of advertising reads: "No advertisement containing an offer to sell a product should be published when the offer is not a bona fide effort to sell the advertised product."[2]

Bait and switch occurs when a store advertises a sale to draw customers into the store and, instead of giving the promised discount, charges regular or slightly higher prices. One good example, on a small scale, of a bait and switch scheme is the so-called used car caper. This version starts with an ad in the newspaper that offers a cheap used car. A car worth $5,000 will be advertised as on sale for $2,500 or less. When you get to the used car lot however you'll find that the car has already been sold, but the salesperson will immediately urge you to test drive another car at a higher price. The whole purpose of the ad was to get you onto the lot. The cheap car depicted in the ad never existed.

If this happens to you, report the dealership—or whatever type of scam it is—immediately to the Better Business Bureau.[3]

FALSE ADVERTISING

It is illegal for manufacturers to use advertising—whether it is in print, on TV, or on the radio—that makes false claims about a product. The ad also may not exaggerate the product's quality or effectiveness.

For example, it is against the law to make a commercial for a new drug that claims it cures a disease unless the drug can actually cure the disease. Con artists make a living selling what used to be called "snake oil," medicines that claim to cure arthritis or cancer, but which are ineffective. Snake oil is a traditional Chinese medicine used to treat joint pain, but the term has come to mean any medicine that is fake or of questionable quality. Today, the rules against false advertising demand that when advertising a prescription drug, the possible side effects have to be mentioned along with the drug's benefits.

Over the years the FTC has taken its share of criticism—when someone is offended by something in an ad, the FTC is often the first to be blamed. But the FTC does not hesitate to take on some big enemies. During the 1960s Shell Oil, with a chain of gas stations across the United States, began to run TV ads claiming that cars drove further on their gas due to a secret ingredient that they called "Platformate." The FTC investigated the claim and discovered that Shell had given the name Platformate to an ingredient found in all commercial gasoline, not just theirs. Although it was true that cars with platformate in the tank drove further than cars with no platformate, gasoline without platformate hadn't been sold anywhere by anyone in many years. Thus, Shell Oil was selling the same gas as the rest of the gas stations, but had invented a key difference as an advertising gimmick. Shell Oil was found guilty of false advertising, was fined, and forced to discontinue the ad campaign.[4]

In the late 1950s and early 1960s, the over-the-counter medicine known as Anacin bragged in its ads that it relieved stress, depression, nervousness, and fatigue. The advertisements also said

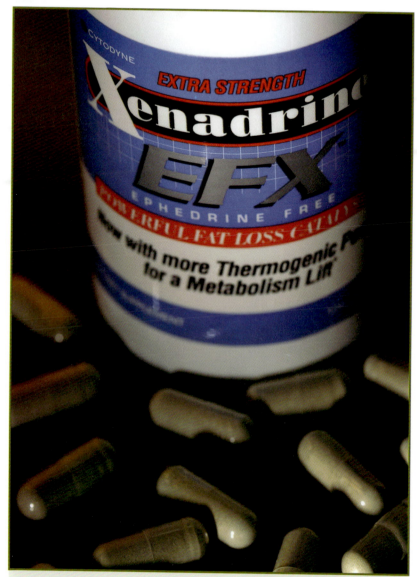

A bottle of Xenadrine EFX capsules. The marketers for this weight-loss product were fined for making false claims about rapid weight loss. *David McNew/Getty Images*

that you could feel the relief only 22 seconds after taking the pill. The FTC soon began an investigation into the product's claims. Anacin, it turned out, wasn't a wonder drug at all, but merely a

QUACKERY: THE STORY OF DUDLEY LEBLANC

Sometimes white-collar criminals are no more than con artists who work on a large scale. One classic example of this was a Louisiana state senator named Dudley J. LeBlanc, who made millions in the years following World War II by selling a "brand new medicine" called Hadacol. In reality, Hadacol was no more than alcohol, vitamin B, and some honey, but it was sold as a miracle drug that cured or helped cure many common diseases such as arthritis and asthma. The "cure-all" sold very well. Because it contained alcohol, it did make people feel better for a little while. Its claim to cure diseases, however, was completely untrue.

In 1951 LeBlanc sold his Hadacol Company for $8 million. After that the popularity of the product decreased. Some local governments had successfully gotten Hadacol treated as a liquor rather than as a medicine, but the fact that LeBlanc's claims regarding Hadacol were fraudulent never resulted in him being arrested.[5]

combination of aspirin and caffeine. And it took a lot longer than 22 seconds for the stomach's acid to break down the pill enough for the chemical to enter the user's system. The FTC also noted that the ads claimed that Anacin was the strongest painkiller available without a prescription and investigation revealed that was not true either.[6]

During the 1980s the FTC had a memorable tussle with the Beech-Nut Nutrition Corporation, makers of baby food. Beech-Nut's ads claimed that their apple juice was "100 percent fruit juice." They also said that the "apple juice" contained no sugar. An analysis by FTC scientists showed that the "apple juice" was loaded with sugar and contained no actual apple juice whatsoever. It was sugar water. The FTC ruling called the juice "a fraudulent chemical cocktail." The prosecution went smoothly and a top Beech-Nut executive pleaded guilty in 1987 of violating federal false-advertising laws.[7]

PRICE GOUGING

The practice of price gouging is proof that some businesspersons are so possessed by greed that they have no shame. They see business as an excuse to put their consciences on the back burner.

The term *price gouging* refers to the greedy practice of unfairly jacking up the price of a product because of an emergency (either real or imagined) or a monopoly. For example, if you tried to charge $10 a glass for clean water in New Orleans in the days after Hurricane Katrina devastated the city, that would be price gouging.

In fact, price gouging happened a lot in the days after that tragedy. Many greedy merchants tripled and quadrupled the price of essential items. Most got away with it, too, because law enforcement was busy with more pressing matters, such as saving people's lives.

Price gouging often occurs along the edges of the law. What is an unfair price? It's a judgment call. Even when price gouging is seemingly obvious, it can be hard to prosecute and convict the guilty parties.

Corporations know that a certain amount of price gouging is allowed because it is so difficult to prove. In one example, the soda companies exploited a sugar shortage during the 1970s, but the government was unable to do anything about it. Because of the sugar shortage, the cost of a soda (Coke, Pepsi, Dr. Pepper, 7UP, etc.) went up a quarter. When the sugar shortage was over, the price did not go back down. The price of diet soda also went up a quarter, even though it contained no sugar.

Sometimes companies get away with price gouging because they believe people are simply willing to pay more. In 1989 all of the major breakfast cereal companies (such as Post, General Mills, Quaker Oats, and Kellogg's) practically doubled their prices within two months of one another, even though there were no reasons (such as a shortage of a key ingredient) to cause that price rise.[8]

One form of gouging is price fixing. This occurs when competitors get together and agree to keep the prices of their products high. Secret signals are often sent back and forth between the companies so that they can raise prices at the same time. A couple of industries where this has been known to happen are the commercial airline business and the oil business. During the 1970s prices skyrocketed in both of those industries because of an "energy crisis." As it turned out, an actual energy crisis didn't exist; rather, it was a scam by the major oil companies. These companies—Exxon, Shell, BP, Gulf, Texaco, Mobil, and Socal (Chevron)—were known as the "Seven Sisters" and they had gotten together to fix the price of gas. The only legal action against the oil companies was a lawsuit brought in 1975 by the citizens of four states (California, Oregon, Washington, and Arizona). The citizens claimed that they had been ripped off by the oil companies because the so-called energy crisis was a conspiracy to raise the price of gas and keep that price high. After 17 years in the courts, the companies began to settle out of court in 1992. They paid out many millions of dollars to get the citizens to drop their lawsuits.[9]

During the early 1990s, the airlines were also accused, in the form of lawsuits, of fixing ticket prices at rates higher than necessary. The airlines involved were American, United, Delta, Northwest, USAir, Continental, TWA, and Alaska. Like the oil companies, they began to pay money back to customers without ever admitting that they were guilty of anything. The airlines ended up "paying back" some of the ticket buyers they'd ripped off with coupons worth 10 percent off the cost of their next flight. The coupons expired in three years and couldn't be used after that. Because the refunds had not come in cash but in what is called "soft money," a coupon or voucher assigned a monetary value, the airlines had gotten away with giving back much less than they had promised.[10]

KNOCKOFFS

Some crooked businesspeople rip off consumers by marketing a product that is less than it seems. In the 1960s and 1970s there was an ad on the inside front cover of many comic books for a "Two-Man Submarine." It cost somewhere in the neighborhood of $5, a lot of money for a kid at the time. When the two-man sub arrived it turned out to be a sheet of plastic with instructions to drape it over a card table. Two kids could then get under the card table and pretend they were in a submarine. Even though common sense told most kids that a two-man sub had to cost more than $5, everyone was disappointed when the product arrived.

In the adult world the result can be a much larger rip-off. One common form of knockoff involves jewelry and purses. The purses are made very cheaply, usually overseas in countries where labor is cheap. The materials are cheap, and the most work goes into

A vendor tries to block photographs being taken of fake Louis Vuitton and Coach brand purses on a street in Beijing in October 2007. Many knockoff products sold in the United States come from China and other foreign countries. *Greg Baker/AP*

making the label a perfect counterfeit of an expensive handbag manufacturer. In other words, a designer label is put on a bargain-basement item. The purses are then sold as if they were really the finest in the world. Another type of knockoff comes in the form of millions of sports-team jerseys sold with official-looking National

Football League or Major League Baseball tags that are, in reality, cheap imitations.

Many knockoff products are manufactured abroad and then smuggled into the United States. Therefore the law enforcement agencies that most often play a role in busting knockoff rings are U.S. Customs and the U.S. Coast Guard. The same organizations that search cargo entering the country for drugs and signs of terrorism also chase down smugglers, including those who are sneaking in counterfeit products.[11]

Crimes Against the Environment:
Love Canal

It didn't take an expert to know that there was something desperately wrong in the tiny community of Love Canal, not far from Buffalo, New York. All one had to do was look around. Too many of the children had horrible birth defects.

One child had a second row of teeth. Another was born with a deformed eye. Another was mentally retarded. Other children had died of leukemia and many expectant mothers lost their babies even before they'd had a chance to give birth. Of course, these things happen, but to have them all occur so frequently in one small neighborhood—well, it was terrifying.

Even before investigators arrived, residents were convinced that the birth defects, child mortality, and miscarriages were being caused by the smelly black glop that kept oozing up from the ground.[1]

Many white-collar criminals make their profits by ignoring laws against polluting the air, land, and water with waste products from manufacturing factories. It is often cheaper to illegally dump industrial waste somewhere than to legally dispose of it, but the consequences of such dumping can be dire.

It is now tougher than ever for companies to get away with causing health hazards with their waste products. Several decades ago, society was still learning environmental lessons the hard way.

The story of what happened at Love Canal is a good example of an environmental crime.

Love Canal was an abandoned waterway not far from Buffalo, New York. From 1942 to 1953 the Hooker Chemical Corporation disposed of millions of pounds of waste by dumping it in Love Canal.[2] The whole area was then filled in with earth and sold for $1 to the local government, which used the land to build an elementary school and a housing project. In 1958 the Hooker Company got an early indication that the dumpsite was hazardous when three boys from the nearby elementary school played with a substance oozing out of a rusty drum, and then had to be treated for burns.

A view of the Niagara Falls Hooker Chemical Plant at sunset on May 23, 1980, in Love Canal, NY. The town closed down as a result of contamination caused by the plant. *Joe Traver/Getty Images*

Hooker paid for the boys' medical treatments and the incident was never officially reported. If there had been a report, Hooker may have been forced to clean up the site, an operation that would have cost the company tens of millions of dollars.

A later investigation turned up a memo from this time from one Hooker executive to another saying that they should not spend any money to clean up Love Canal unless they were specifically asked to do so by the local school board. For reasons that remain unclear today, the local school board never made that request, not until it was too late and the community was changed forever.[3]

THE COST OF CRIME

Later studies showed that, over the next 20 years, the children of Love Canal were sicker and grew to be smaller than kids from neighboring communities. Lois Gibbs, a Love Canal housewife, became a spokesperson for the victims, saying, "We had no idea that we were living on top of a chemical graveyard."[4]

Gibbs first became active in the cause after reading about the history of Love Canal in a local newspaper. She realized that her young son had been sick ever since he started attending the Love Canal school. She tried to get him transferred to another school, and when this didn't work, she went door to door with a petition to close the school. As she talked to her neighbors, petition in hand, she discovered that most of the children were sick. With a small army of local parents behind her, she went on to lead a campaign to call attention to the neighborhood.

Her activism led the New York State Health Commissioner, in the spring of 1978, to declare the Love Canal area hazardous. There could be no denying the direct link between the illness-causing chemicals that saturated the Love Canal environment and the actual illnesses that were being experienced there. Of the 80 chemical compounds found to be oozing through the ground at Love Canal, scientists found 12 of them to be cancer-causing.[5] The school was closed and many families were evacuated. This, in turn, got the attention of President Jimmy Carter, who brought in the resources of the federal government. It is difficult to determine

(continues)

(continued)

the ultimate cost of the Love Canal disaster to taxpayers. People needed to be relocated, the land cleaned up, and health care provided. Estimates at the time were that the Love Canal disaster would cost more than $250 million.[6]

Lois Gibbs, a former Love Canal resident and community leader, speaks on August 1, 2003, to commemorate the 25th anniversary of the discovery of the toxic waste landfill under the town. *Harry Scull Jr./Getty Images*

In 1977 the spring thaw caused the chemicals under the ground at Love Canal to seep into the basements of homes in the community. People who found the stuff oozing into their homes like a black sludge did not know how deadly the material was. Tests showed the leaking substance was made of dioxin, one of the world's strongest poisons, and benzene, a strong cancer-causing substance. According to the Environmental Protection Agency (EPA), even very small amounts of benzene can cause cancer. At Love Canal large amounts of benzene were present in the soil and seeping out. Soon women who lived in the area stopped having healthy pregnancies. Of 16 pregnancies there in 1979, only one healthy baby was born. Many died. The others were deformed.

If an individual had been physically attacking pregnant women in the Love Canal area and causing them to lose babies or to have sick babies, police would have hunted the perpetrator, and if caught and convicted, he or she would have been imprisoned. Because the crimes were against the environment, U.S. President Jimmy Carter declared the Love Canal area a disaster area, and the Federal Disaster Assistance Agency was called in to investigate and to help clean up the mess. The EPA sent in investigators. Federal government lawmakers formed a subcommittee. One member of the House of Representatives subcommittee investigating Love Canal was future vice president and environmentalist, Al Gore, who "condemned" the actions of the Hooker Chemical Corporation, and observed that the horror of Love Canal could have been avoided if the company had heeded early warnings of the danger.[7]

The federal government saw to it that the Love Canal site was cleaned up, although by that time some of the damage to the area's ecology was permanent. It was not until 1995, 18 years after the sludge began to ooze, that Occidental Petroleum, the parent company of Hooker Chemicals, agreed to pay the government $129 million for having cleaned up Love Canal.

One would expect that the corporation learned a lesson because of Love Canal and began disposing of waste safely and legally. But it didn't. The government's punishment to the company failed to change Hooker's behavior. In 1990 the corporation again fell into legal trouble, this time because of waste illegally disposed of on Long Island. Once again dioxin was among the chemicals being dumped.[8]

Health Care,
Bad Investments,
and Spam

White-collar crimes often occur in the financial and health care industries. The police have methods for dealing with such crimes in both industries, and there are also steps individuals can take for investing safely and avoiding traps and schemes to steal their money.

HEALTH CARE FRAUD

On July 18, 2006, Bradley J. Schlozman, the Kansas City, Missouri, District Attorney, told the public that a federal grand jury had called for the arrest of 13 women. They were accused of committing fraud by stealing $120,000 from a health care benefit program. The crimes had taken place in 2002 and were an inside job, meaning someone working in the benefit program helped carry out the theft.

The apparent ringleader was 37-year-old Cheri Smith. The scheme worked like this: Smith took a job working for Health Midwest Comprehensive Care (HMCC). She was a senior team leader responsible for data entry of all pharmacy claims. Using her position, she gained access to a computer database and added to the list of those receiving benefits the names of many of her family members and friends. The people whose names had been added to the list began receiving checks they didn't deserve.[1]

On October 10, 2006, Smith pleaded guilty to health care fraud. On March 30, 2007, Smith was sentenced by U.S. District Judge Howard F. Sachs to three years and four months in federal prison without parole.[2] The other women pleaded guilty as well, but have not yet been sentenced.

The scheme's flaw was that those receiving checks were not members of the insurance plan. When FBI computer experts ran a routine check (also called "data mining") of those receiving checks against a list of those eligible for checks, it revealed the names of those illegally receiving money. One recipient, Sandra Rivers, was questioned by the FBI and admitted to receiving checks to which she was not entitled.[3]

Doctors sometimes commit insurance fraud, billing for procedures that were not performed or were unnecessary. Other health care frauds include making up false bills or overbilling for transportation services (ambulances, ambulettes, etc.), and Medicare/Medicaid.

Computer checks by the Department of Justice's Health Care Fraud and Abuse Control Program of the claims physicians send to insurance companies can pick out charges and frequency-of-treatments that are out of the ordinary. If a doctor is charging five times what another doctor in the same region is charging for the same service, yet he has just as many or more customers, then insurance investigators know something might be wrong. If a dentist is cleaning the same patient's teeth once a week when other dentists are only doing this procedure once every six months, the computer flags this as unusual and the dentist might be investigated. If the dentist is found to be charging for made-up or unnecessary procedures, he or she will be charged with fraud.

INVESTMENT FRAUD

Investment fraud is at the heart of the movie—and the Broadway musical comedy—*The Producers*. The story is simple. A pair of theater producers use their contacts with the wealthy to sell a percentage of the profits of a forthcoming show in order to raise money for the production. Each investor buys a percentage of the show, and although only 100 percent exists, the producers continue to sell parts of the show past the 100 percent mark. Each contributor believes he or she will receive a quarter or a half of the profits, but there are 30 of them, making this impossible. The producers have amassed a fortune by taking everyone's money. They then set out to find the worst play of all time, which turns out to be a musical titled *Springtime for Hitler*. They want the play to flop so that there won't be any profits to be divided, allowing the producers to close the show and escape with the money. Unfortunately for them, the musical turns out to be a smash hit and they are ruined when their many contributors want their profits.

A real-life white-collar criminal might avoid the producers' mistake of actually creating a product. They should have fled the country to South America and forgotten about putting on their musical before anyone realized what had happened. That's the method used by some real-world criminals.

This type of investment fraud is common, and it is never as funny as it is in *The Producers*. In 2003 five people were arrested in Portland, Oregon, and charged with fraud and money laundering. They were accused of stealing more than $100 million by convincing their victims to deposit and invest money in imaginary banks by promising that these banks had $74 billion in assets and "guaranteeing" investors a 300 percent annual return from their investment. The ringleaders of the scheme—Robert J. Skirving and Rita L. Regale—pleaded guilty in July 2006. Skirving received an eight-year prison sentence. Regale was given 18 months behind bars. The others' sentences averaged about five-years in prison each.

Authorities first became aware of the fraud when duped investors complained that they were not receiving the money they had been promised. It is an old rule of small-time con artists that the key to getting away with the crime is to get away from the victims before they realize they have been had. The case was broken through eight years of international investigation, obtaining records from banks in the United States, Grenada, Austria, and Uganda. The investigation was successful because of the teamwork of the Criminal Investigation Department of the Internal Revenue Service (IRS) and the FBI. The IRS is the federal organization that collects income taxes. Many white-collar criminals have been caught because he or she failed to file an honest tax return.

TAX CHEATS

Tax fraud makes up a large percentage of white-collar crime. It comes in two forms. Some are committed by people who don't pay all of the taxes they owe to their state or federal government. The other consists of crimes committed by those who steal from programs paid for by tax dollars. The Government Accountability Office has estimated that as much as 10 percent of the tax dollars spent on government programs don't make it to their intended targets because of fraud.[4] Much of this fraud exploits U.S. health care programs, but other government programs have been subject to scams as well. In the military, money set aside to pay for equipment or soldiers' salaries has been known to disappear. Every year members of the U.S. military are court-martialed (receive a military trial) for committing fraud, bribery, and taking kickbacks. On a smaller scale, school administrators have been known to take taxpayers' money set aside to buy books and equipment for students, and put it in their own pockets.

Alan LeBouidge, commissioner of the Massachusetts Department of Revenue, poses inside the command center in March 2004. State revenue agencies nationwide are using new high-tech methods such as data mining to catch tax evaders. *Lisa Poole/AP*

There was a time when cooperation between various governmental agencies, including those involved in law enforcement, was rare. A criminal, for example, could easily get away with a crime by simply crossing a state line. This is no longer the case. In this high-technology world, it is not uncommon for the FBI to use the resources of other agencies, such as the IRS, to help bring criminals to justice—just as today criminals crossing state lines often run into cops waiting for them on the other side.

IRS computers scan for those who don't file a tax return at all, those who take false deductions from their taxable income, and those who spend more money than they earn. This last group sometimes includes people who are not reporting all of the money they make to the government. Frequently these tax cheats are found to be committing other forms of white-collar crime.[5] To cover up money gained from illegal activities, such as embezzling or fraud, they don't report it to the IRS.

SPAM SCAMS

Spam is unsolicited mass e-mail sent to advertise products or events, or to lure people into scams. Spam used to commit stock fraud is an updated version of what used to be called "the telephone boiler-room scam." The con artist buys many shares in a stock that is selling at a very low price, perhaps $1 a share. The person then starts making phone calls, often just picking numbers out of the phone book. They tell the potential victims (also known as "the marks") that the stock is on the verge of going up to $20 a share by the end of the month so they should get in on the deal, and get in quick. The con then offers the mark the shares for only $10 apiece. If the con artist has purchased 1,000 shares and sells them all over the phone, he brings in $9,000. That's the boiler-room scam, also known as the "ol' pump and dump." The con artist pumps up the product and then dumps it on the mark for an inflated price. Con artists sometimes fill rooms with phones and have employees make phone call after phone call, telling blatant lies to sell the stock at an unreasonable price, until all the stock is gone.

Con artists have updated the scam for the Internet age. Now, using spam techniques, they send e-mails to thousands of recipients simultaneously. If only a small percentage buy the stock, a big profit can be made.

Among the claims often used in such scams are

- The stock is going to "explode" in value. The mark is often told a projected price that the stock will reach within a very short period of time.
- According to the *New York Daily News*, the marks are sometimes made to feel like they have received the e-mail by mistake and that it contains "inside information" that they were not intended to see. The e-mail might start, "Hey Jim, I made a lot of money for you last time. Here's another sure thing." In reality, there is no "Jim," but the mark doesn't know that.
- There will almost always be some claim that previous picks have all turned out to be winners, and listed will be "before and after" prices of so-called previous predictions, almost always regarding either made up stocks or made up prices.

Some marks who know the spam campaign is a scam might go for it anyway under the theory that the stock's price will actually go up because of the spam campaign, and, as long as they sell their stock before the price collapses, they can still make money. This can work if the mark is one of the first to react to the spam, experts say, but the great majority of people who invest in these schemes end up losing money.

According to Purdue University professor of portfolio management, Laura Frieder, even if one buys the stock on the day that it is being most heavily touted by spam, and sells it two days later, the investor still, on the average, will lose 5.5 percent of their money.[6] Because the con artists do not use stocks that belong to the major exchanges and never deal in high volume investment, many investors find that there is no one to sell their stock to when they decide to get rid of it.[7]

Most Internet servers these days use spam filters to weed out e-mails that appear to be spam. According to spam expert Richard Cox, expert spammers use a technique called Bayesian Poisoning to fool the filters.[8] They include with the spam text blocks of gibberish designed to fool spam filters and trick servers into believing the spam is a legitimate e-mail. Some spam messages come with a virus attached so that upon opening the message the e-mail is automatically forwarded to everyone on that recipient's e-mail list.

Cox said, "Your computer could be spreading the e-mail and you might not even notice."

Despite the sophistication of the authorities and anti-spam and anti-fraud forces, there are few arrests. It can be difficult to pinpoint the origin of spam, but not impossible.

According to John Reed Stark, the chief of the Securities and Exchange Commission's Office of Internet Enforcement, headquartered in Washington, D.C., "We can trace the e-mail, and secondly, whenever anyone makes any money on the stock, we're going to find out about it."[10] One trouble with making arrests is that the scammers often move from place to place, both in terms of their geographical location and their Internet address. Experts point out to anyone thinking of attempting this spam technique, that anyone who uses spam to manipulate the price of a stock is breaking the law.

Experts say that the best advice to people is to never invest money with a stranger calling on the phone, and always delete e-mail that comes from an address you don't recognize.

Stark also says, "When I see spams go around, I think investors should look at them like a flyer on your windshield and throw them out right away."

RULES TO REMEMBER

To protect yourself against spam fraud, here are some techniques recommended by the *Daily News*:

- Protect your computer with security software like firewalls and anti-spam filters, and update them frequently. Good firewalls and filters can block most spam e-mails.
- If spam does get through, *never respond*. Not even to tell the spammer off. By responding you are allowing the spammer to learn things about you and your computer.
- Never follow a link from an e-mail that was sent to you by someone you do not know.
- Never provide any personal or financial details in response to a spam e-mail.[9]

Because of our freedom-of-speech rights, legislators cannot ban spam entirely, but they can pass laws to limit the amount of damage spam can do. First and foremost among these laws is the humorously named Can-Spam Act, which became a federal law in 2003. This law requires that all e-mails that are intended to sell something must be labeled as such. It is illegal, therefore, to disguise a sales pitch with the e-mail title "Mom Sends Her Love." All spam must correctly identify the sender. And those who receive spam must always have the option of not opening the e-mail if they don't want to.[11]

Some states have their own laws limiting what spammers can do as well.

Corporate Crime:
Enron

Imagine you are a hard worker who has spent decades working for the same company. Every two weeks you get a paycheck, a portion of which has been taken out and invested. The idea is that, when you turn 65 years old and it is time for you to retire, you will cash in those investments and have plenty of money with which to live out the rest of your life.

You have spent many years dreaming of retirement. You know just where you are going to move. You have imagined the places to which you would travel on long vacations. But, when the time comes to actually retire and you seek the money that you've been saving and investing, you are horrified to find that it is gone.

It turns out that the whole "investment" operation was a gigantic scam. You and many of your coworkers have been robbed of your retirement funds. That money, it seems, went straight from your paycheck into the pockets of the executives running the company, the company you trusted.

Sound impossible? Well, it isn't. It has happened.

Corporate crimes occur when executives working for large corporations use their jobs to funnel large amounts of money from the company they work for into their own pockets. This type of crime hurts society in several ways:

1. It steals money from investors.
2. It erodes public trust.
3. It costs the public money.

All corporate crime is a financial drain on society. It costs everyone money because non-investors often help pay the price of the crime through higher consumer prices and interest rates. Other smaller businesses may have to close, and honest workers end up losing their jobs. There's a ripple effect to corporate crime, the size of which depends on the size of the criminal corporation.

The most famous case of corporate crime in recent years is the Enron case. The company was founded by Kenneth Lay in Omaha, Nebraska, in 1985. Enron later moved its headquarters to Houston, Texas.

Enron was born out of the merger of three companies, two gas and electric companies and a railroad. Its business was energy. At its peak it employed 21,000 people and dealt in many different fields, including electricity, natural gas, pulp and paper, and communications. It was the seventh largest company in the United States, claiming to be worth $101 billion. *Fortune* magazine called

STEPPING UP THE WAR ON CORPORATE CRIME

Here are some ways law enforcement and the government are better at fighting corporate crime than they were a generation ago. They

- better learn to determine when corporate crimes have occurred. Much of this new capability is technological. Computer whizzes working for law enforcement have to be just a little bit smarter than those using the computers to commit crimes.
- have the resources to investigate and prosecute all corporate fraud. More money is available today to combat corporate crime. Some of this money is paid by taxpayers, but still more comes from the hefty fines white-collar criminals now have to pay when they are caught.
- have increased the punishment, both in terms of fines and prison sentences, of those convicted of corporate crimes. White-collar criminals who once could have gotten away with simply paying a fine even when caught now find themselves facing serious prison terms.

Enron employees remove their belongings in boxes from Enron
Headquarters after being laid off due to the collapse of the company.
Greg Smith/Corbis

it "America's Most Innovative Company" for six straight years (1996–2001).

Enron was indeed innovative. Here's an example. It was the first corporation that allowed investors to trade its stock online. If investors wanted to put their life savings into Enron's future, all that was needed was a click of the mouse.

But Enron fell apart in December 2001 when it was revealed that just about all of the company's supposed money and possessions were made up—pure fiction.

Enron had accountants who made it look like the company was making money by the billions, when in reality the company was deeply in debt. When the company finally collapsed, with it went $60 billion worth of stocks purchased by investors, now worthless.

Also gone was another couple billion dollars in pension funds—the money that was to pay the pension for Enron's employees. So, in many cases, faithful Enron employees were the ones who were burned the worst by this heinous crime.

Where did all the money go at Enron? Straight to the top, apparently, considering who was later arrested and prosecuted. In September 2004 Andrew Fastow, Enron's formal chief financial officer, and, according to the Associated Press, "one of the key figures in Enron Corp.'s collapse," was sentenced to six years in prison.[1]

Fastow was sentenced to 10 years in prison in 2004, but two years later the judge shortened the sentence by four years. U.S. District Judge Kenneth Hoyt said that society had unfairly picked on Fastow's family and that they all had "suffered enough." Fastow's wife, Lea, also pleaded guilty in 2004 to a misdemeanor tax crime and served a year in prison for helping to hide ill-gotten gains from her husband's schemes.

Judge Hoyt said that the facts "called for mercy." At the hearing, the convicted white-collar criminal was allowed to give his wife a hug before he was handcuffed and led away.

"I know I deserve punishment," Fastow said, as he exited. "I accept it without bitterness."[2]

Also prosecuted for their part in the bilking of the huge corporation were the company's founder, Kenneth Lay, and the company's former chief executive officer, Jeffrey Skilling. One of the reasons the court believed that Fastow deserved "mercy" was that he had been willing to testify against the other two men at their trials, stating under oath that both Lay and Skilling knew about the phony accounting practices that made Enron appear to be so much richer than it actually was.

Former Enron CFO Andrew Fastow leaves the federal courthouse in shackles after receiving a six-year sentence for corporate fraud. *Aaron M. Sprecher/epa/Corbis*

♀ POWER TO THE PEOPLE

The Enron employees who were rooked out of their pensions got together and formed the Severed Enron Employee Coalition, which worked to retrieve money from the men they accused of stealing it. The group of more than 20,000 former employees got their money back by filing a lawsuit against the corporation. They charged that the misdeeds of executives in the corporation had cost them the value of their Enron stock ownership and 401(k) plans. They were awarded $89 million dollars, and many of the former employees received their first checks in 2007. Unfortunately, a computer problem caused some people to receive too much money, causing further delays and legal woes while the error was corrected.[3]

In May 2006 both Lay and Skilling were convicted on charges of conspiracy (working with others to commit a crime) and fraud. Before Lay could serve prison time, however, he died of heart disease. Skilling was sentenced to 24 years in the Federal Correctional Institution in Waseca, Minnesota. Fastow had been charged on 98 counts, including fraud, insider trading, and money laundering. He pleaded guilty to two counts of conspiracy and admitted to running schemes to hide Enron debt and inflate profits. He did this, he admitted, while keeping his own coffers filled with cash at all times. As part of his guilty plea, Fastow agreed to give back nearly $30 million in cash and property.

The first party to face criminal charges following Enron's collapse was Arthur Andersen LLP, the accounting firm that had been hired to check Enron's books and had ruled that everything was on the up and up.[4]

Arthur Andersen was tried and found guilty of obstruction of justice. It is against the law to know a crime has been committed and choose not to report it to authorities. It is also against the law to obstruct justice by lying to a federal investigator. In addition to simply ignoring the problems they found in Enron's books, Arthur Andersen was accused of actively hiding the crimes. When the firm knew that an investigation was coming, they shredded thousands of revealing documents and also destroyed a memo from one Enron executive to another that would have revealed large-scale white-collar crime.

From a law enforcement standpoint, the prosecution of one of the nation's "Big Five" accounting firms sent a powerful message to the many accountants who worked for companies across the nation. It was their responsibility to tell if they knew there was illegal business going on, and if they refused to inform authorities, they would be punished.

Computer Crimes and ID Theft

It is lucky that, thus far, computer hackers have been mostly mischievous rather than evil. One of the most famous computer hackers was Kevin Mitnick.[1] In fact, he was a highly publicized computer whiz even before he got into trouble.

KEVIN MITNICK: HACKER EXTRAORDINAIRE

Mitnick was arrested after what Assistant U.S. Attorney Christopher Painter called "a countrywide hacking spree" that earned Mitnick a spot on the FBI's Most Wanted list. Over a two-and-a-half-year period, Mitnick allegedly hacked into computers, stole corporate secrets, scrambled phone networks, broke into the national defense warning system, and caused millions of dollars in losses. The FBI arrested Mitnick in 1995.

"He's a danger to the community," said Painter following Mitnick's arrest. "We're talking about someone who has consistently and without self-control hacked into systems everywhere. He also was a fugitive and used multiple identities. We think there's a firm basis for holding him, and the courts have agreed."[2]

Mitnick served five years in prison after pleading guilty to charges of wire and computer fraud. He was released in 2000 and today runs a computer security firm.

Mitnick, to this day, denies that he did some of the things of which he was accused. He admits that he broke into corporate computer systems and stole computer programming source code. He says he did it to satisfy his own curiosity, to see if it could be done, and not to make money. He denies that he hacked into NORAD (the North American Aerospace Defense Command) or that he wiretapped the FBI.

In 2005 Mitnick told CNN, "Claims that I wiretapped the FBI or something like that were something out of a movie like *War Games* or *Enemy of the State* or something. There were fictional events that were tied to real events, like when I took code from Motorola and Nokia when I was a hacker to look at the source code. I took a copy, which is essentially stealing, to look at the information."

Although he takes responsibility for getting himself into trouble, he blames a story in the *New York Times* that made him appear dangerous for much of his trouble. After that article was published, Mitnick says, the government investigation into his activities went into high gear.

"At the end of the day, I would have been prosecuted, but I wouldn't have been held in solitary confinement for a year for the fear that I could launch nuclear missiles by whistling through a pay phone.

"I was powerless because I was represented by a publicly appointed attorney who had a very limited budget. But a lot of accusations I wasn't charged with. If I hacked into NORAD or wiretapped the FBI, I certainly would have been charged with it," he said.

Mitnick says today he uses his powers only for good. Since hacking into computer systems was his greatest skill, he earns his living today telling corporations how to prevent hackers from getting into their system. He gives speeches to security experts and sometimes visits corporations and examines their computer systems so he can best advise them.

"People hire me to break into their systems to find their security failures and patch them before the bad guys find them," Mitnick says.

Mitnick is happy in his work. He gets to practice the same sort of criminal activity he did before, but now he doesn't have to worry about getting caught.

"It is really rewarding to know that I can take my background and skills and knowledge and really help the community," he says.

¶ OPERATION FIREWALL

During the autumn of 2004, after a yearlong investigation, the United States Secret Service arrested 28 suspects in eight U.S. states and six foreign countries on charges of identity theft, computer fraud, credit card fraud, and conspiracy. The investigation that led to the arrests was headed by the Secret Service, but was actually a joint effort involving many local law enforcement agencies within the United States, as well as those in the Ukraine, the Netherlands, Sweden, Poland, Belarus, and Bulgaria. The investigation began when the agencies started monitoring visitors to several credit card theft sites online (such as cvv.ru, virgindumps.com, and shadowcrew.com). These sites taught those who visited how to launder money, break into databases, and steal identities. Investigators used phony screen names and online identities to gain the trust of those operating the Web sites. Investigators learned that the Web sites could provide "entire wallets" of fake ID for those willing to pay the high price. After months of online correspondence, one of the administrators of the Shadowcrew Web site sent an e-mail to an investigator that was traceable. The administrator was arrested and provided information to the investigators that led to the other arrests.[4]

The suspects were found to have stolen 1.7 million credit card numbers. Using those numbers, they had stolen more than $4.3 million. If the gang had not been broken up so quickly, the amount stolen could have rapidly grown into the hundreds of millions.

The director of the Secret Service, W. Ralph Basham, said about the arrests: "Information is the world's new currency. These suspects targeted to personal and financial information of ordinary citizens (and) to companies engaged in e-commerce."[5]

The arrested suspects comprised three cybercrime rings known as Darkprofits, Carderplanet, and Shadowcrew. They ran Web sites that trafficked in credit card numbers and fake identification cards. The Web sites offered, for a fee, fake passports and fake birth certificates.[6]

Mitnick described for CNN how a hacker had gotten access to Paris Hilton's cell phone numbers, the point being that, if someone could do that to a show business celebrity, they could also do it to a high-ranking member of the U.S. intelligence community and national secrets could be compromised.[3]

As another example, Mitnick discussed the Internal Revenue Service, the people who collect federal taxes. They did a study to see how secure their systems were and found out that the answer was, not that secure. Researchers posing as technical support workers called 100 managers. Of those managers, 35 freely gave the caller key passwords and user names over the phone. The study was meaningful. A company can spend millions of dollars trying to keep its secrets safe, but it only takes one employee who is too quick to trust the wrong person and all of those security measures are wasted.

IDENTITY THEFT

What Paris Hilton suffered at the hands of hackers is called *identity theft* or *ID theft*. This crime occurs when someone uses deception or theft to learn another person's key information, such as computer passwords, credit card numbers, or social security number.

An identification thief does not have to break into a home to steal money. They may steal a victim's key numbers by standing behind them and peeking over their shoulder while they are using a cash machine.

Sometimes these thieves do what is called *dumpster diving*. They go through garbage cans and public dumpsters searching for checks, credit card or bank statements, or other records that bear a name, address, and telephone number.

Some thieves call their victims on the phone and pretend to be someone they aren't. Using some sort of scam they ask for the key numbers, and the victims freely give them. This same technique is also common using the Internet instead of the telephone.

No matter how thieves get the numbers, once they have them they can quickly purchase items and charge them to the victim, or, even worse, empty out the victim's bank accounts. Someone who suspects that his or her identity has been stolen must act quickly. The longer one waits, the more damage can be done, and the harder it will be to fix it. When victims of identity theft call

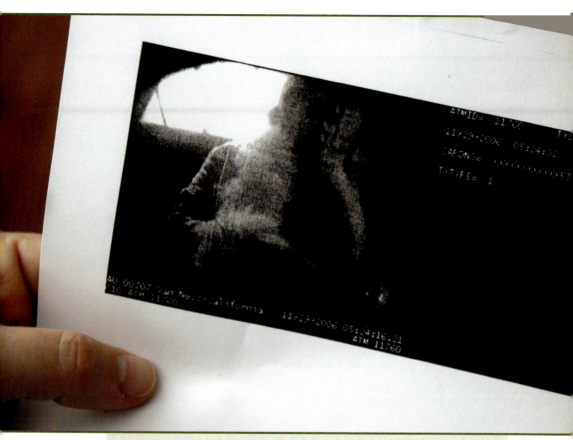

A victim of identity theft holds her bank's photograph of an alleged suspect using an ATM to withdraw funds from her accounts. *Michael Macor/San Francisco Chronicle/Corbis*

the authorities and make other important phone calls regarding the theft, they should keep a written log of the time of each call, the phone number called, with whom they spoke, and what was said. When possible, he or she should confirm conversations in writing and keep copies of all written communications. Keeping track of any expenses incurred while trying to fix the problem might help in recovering that money if the thief is caught.

Anyone whose credit cards or numbers have been stolen should immediately contact the major credit recording companies: Experian (888) EXPERIAN, Equifax (800) 525-6285, and Trans Union (800) 680-7289. Victims of identity theft should report the theft, request a free credit report, and request that their file to be flagged with a fraud alert. He or she should make these contacts both on the phone and in writing and not pay any bill for any goods or services that weren't received. Next, the victim should carefully read their credit report and get in touch with all creditors with whom fraud has been committed and fill out affidavits. Blank affidavits are available to fill out at https://rn.ftc.gov/pls/dod/widtpubl$.startup?Z_ORG_CODE=PU03. An affidavit is a written statement made under oath. This assures that the writer is telling the truth, since it is against the law to lie while under oath (perjury). In a sense, filling out an affidavit is like a written form of testifying in court.

Targets of identity theft should next contact local police to report the crime and request a copy of all police reports. Police may request the credit report indicating the fraud, which is why it is necessary to contact the credit recording companies first.

Those who have had checks stolen should call their bank and put stop payments on any outstanding checks, cancel all their bank accounts, and open new ones. In the same vein, if an ATM card has been stolen, it must be canceled immediately and replaced with a new one. Cardholders should use a new and different password, one that cannot be easily guessed by someone who knows your birthday, social security number, or other personal information. The same is true of phone service. Victims of identity theft should change their phone accounts and passwords.[7]

Insider Trading:
The Case
of Martha Stewart

Insider trading laws prohibit anyone from using their knowledge of goings on within a company to gain profit by buying or selling the company's stock. The most interesting thing about the insider trading laws is that very few people have ever been convicted of breaking them.

According to *Capitalism Magazine*, "The feds have rarely been successful in cases against recipients of inside information. In two of the most famous examples—the 1980 case against Vincent Chiarella, who worked for a financial printer, and the 1983 case against analyst Ray Dirks, who . . . told his clients about an insurance scandal he had uncovered—convictions were overturned by the U.S. Supreme Court."[1] But one person who was convicted of charges related to insider trading and did do time behind bars was Martha Stewart, the popular TV personality and homemaking guru.

HOUSEWIFE TURNED MEDIA MOGUL

Martha Stewart was once chief executive of a homemaking media empire, which included several television shows and a successful magazine production business. A former model and Connecticut housewife, Stewart went from running a modest catering business to making millions of dollars by showing people how to do

⚲ REPORTING FRAUD

The government polices abuses of federal funds through its Government Accountability Office (GAO). The wing of that office that deals with complaints and information from the public is FraudNET. The people at FraudNET review the information they receive from the public, and, when they decide it is believable and sufficient for further action, they relay the information to the GAO's Forensic Audits and Special Investigations Team. To report fraud, waste, abuse, or mismanagement of federal funds, go to FraudNET at http://www.gao.gov/fraudnet/fraudnet.htm, e-mail fraudnet@gao.gov, fax 202-512-3086, or write to GAO FraudNET, 441 G Street NW, Washington DC 20548. Informants' confidentiality is guaranteed.

everything from baking a cake to refinishing furniture. Her motto was, "It's a good thing." She was a media personality with enormous star power when, in 2002, she was investigated on insider trading charges.

Stewart was the kind of celebrity who evoked strong emotions in people. Some people loved her, but many did not. Because of her keen attention to detail she was seen by some to be persnickety and aloof.

Her fans could tell that she got her own joke. She understood that her need for everything to be just-so was a lifestyle for only a few, but it served as a source of entertainment for many. The part of the public that didn't get the show business aspect of Stewart's work tended to not like Stewart. They thought she should lighten up.

QUESTIONABLE BUSINESS DEALINGS

The public's opinions were also mixed when it came to light that Stewart was being investigated for shady investment practices. According to *Capitalism Magazine*, the government believed that on December 27, 2001, Stewart had learned from her broker that Samuel Waksal, the chief executive of ImClone Systems, Inc., was trying to sell his stock. Waksal was selling because the FDA

Former CEO of ImClone Systems Sam Waksal speaks to the House Energy and Commerce Committee's investigations subcommittee on Capitol Hill in Washington in June 2002. Waksal pled guilty to multiple charges in the company's insider trading case involving Martha Stewart. *Reuters/Corbis*

was about to announce a decision that would cost the corporation money and be discouraging to future investors.

Stewart, who owned ImClone stock, decided to sell it immediately, knowing that she would get a better price for her shares than if she sold them after news of the FDA's decision became public. To be specific, she sold her 3,928 shares for $58 apiece. Then the news of the FDA's decision became public. The decision involved bad news regarding an anticancer drug ImClone was trying to market.

Once the story made the papers, ImClone's stock fell in value as expected. Soon it was selling for only $45 a share. That meant that Stewart had saved herself $50,000 because she was an "insider" and knew what was going to happen before the rest of the public did.

To many this seems like keen investing, that being smarter than your competitors is one of the key ways to win in a capitalist system. But the government disagreed, holding that Stewart had broken insider trading laws.

Some argued that Stewart was not guilty of any crime. They maintained that insider trading laws were designed to punish corporate insiders who used their knowledge to betray the trust stockholders place in them. If Martha Stewart had been a high-ranking official within ImClone then she would have been guilty. But she was merely an investor with friends in powerful places. The other argument against her committing a crime was that there didn't seem to be a victim.

The investor who purchased her shares at $58 per share would have gotten a better deal if he or she had waited a couple of days. But that investor was prepared to purchase ImClone on that day and didn't care whose shares were purchased. If Stewart had not made her shares available that day, the investor would have purchased them from someone else.

INSIDER TRADING CHARGES

On June 4, 2003, Stewart was charged with both criminal and civil insider trading violations. The criminal charges were not exactly for insider trading. Stewart was charged with the lesser crime of lying to officials when they first asked her about the sale of her ImClone stock.

"This criminal case is about lying, lying to the FBI, lying to the SEC and lying to investors," James B. Comey, the U.S. Attorney for the Southern District of New York, told a news conference on June 4, 2003. "This is conduct that will not be tolerated by anybody."[2]

The investigation also revealed evidence that Stewart had committed securities fraud. She was charged with making false statements regarding her own company. These statements, the charges said, defrauded investors by causing the price of the stock to rise well beyond what it was worth.

The charges were so severe that, if found guilty of them all, Stewart could have faced a 30-year prison sentence. (Stewart was 61 years old at the time.)

A closer look at the fraud charge made it seem less harsh. The charges were, specifically, that she lied when she said she was innocent of the other charges to keep the price of her own company's stock high. Of course, she had yet to be convicted of anything and was presumed innocent. The possibility still existed that Stewart denied the federal charges against her not to manipulate the price of a stock, but because those charges were false.

In order to get a conviction on the fraud charge the prosecution would have to first show that Stewart was indeed lying when she said she was innocent, and then prove that she had done it to keep the price of her own company's stock from going down. It seemed unlikely that both proofs could be made in a court of law, and a judge threw out the charge before Stewart went to trial.[3]

Those critical of the long and pricey investigation into Stewart noted that the investigation was costing the taxpayers tens of times more than Stewart's $51,000 profit. Other white-collar crimes were much larger but, because the defendants were rich but relatively unknown corporate bigwigs, those cases didn't receive nearly as much publicity as the Stewart case. CNN noted that "Dennis Kozlowski and Mark Swartz are charged with looting Tyco of $600 million, John Rigas and his sons are charged with stealing millions from Adelphia, the cable company Rigas founded, and the collapse of Enron and WorldCom led to billions of dollars in losses for investors and costs thousands their jobs."[4] These cases did not receive the same level of media attention as did Martha Stewart's.

After her arrest Stewart immediately stepped down as the chairperson and chief executive officer of her own corporation, Martha Stewart Living Omnimedia. The civil charges were from a lawsuit brought by the Securities and Exchange Commission.

Martha Stewart, found guilty of lying to investigators about a suspicious stock sale, and her lawyer leave federal court in New York on March 5, 2004. *CHIP EAST/Reuters/Corbis*

In 2004 Stewart was found guilty after a long and highly pub-licized trial in New York City. A jury listened to testimony for five weeks and then found Martha Stewart guilty on four counts of obstructing justice and lying to investigators about a well-timed stock sale.

The case was important because it showed that the government was serious about insider trading laws. "The word is *beware*—and don't engage in this type of conduct because it will not be tolerated," David Kelley, U.S. Attorney for the Southern District of New York, said outside the courthouse.

One of the jurors said, "This is a victory for the little guys. No one is above the law."

After her conviction Stewart posted the following statement on her Web site: "Dear Friends: I am obviously distressed by the jury's verdict but I take comfort in knowing that I have done nothing wrong and that I have the enduring support of my family and friends. I believe in the fairness of the judicial system and remain confident that I will ultimately prevail."[5]

PRISON SENTENCE

On the day of her sentencing, a huge crowd gathered outside the courthouse in lower Manhattan, all seeking a glimpse of Stewart. She received the minimum sentence. She had to spend five months in prison and another five months of home confinement. She had to stay at home and wore a bracelet around her ankle that alerted authorities if she strayed too far off of her own property.[6]

After hearing her sentence, Stewart said, "I'll be back. I will be back. I'm used to all kinds of hard work, as you know, and I'm not afraid. I'm not afraid whatsoever."

Before the sentencing, Stewart told Judge Miriam Goldman Cedarbaum, "This is a shameful day." She called the charges "a small personal matter" that became "an almost fatal circus event."

She shot prosecutor Karen Patton Seymour a nasty glare when the assistant district attorney said, "Citizens like Ms. Stewart, who willingly take the steps to lie to officials when they are under investigation about their own conduct, should not expect leniency."

Stewart served her time and after her release made good-natured jokes about her time behind bars. Perhaps the most surprising thing about the whole affair came when Stewart rather seamlessly resumed her life as a TV star. The public, if it thought she was guilty of anything at all, apparently forgave her.

Stewart's final punishment came in 2006 when she finally settled her lawsuit with the Securities and Exchange Commission for $195,000. Along with the payment she agreed not to serve as the director of a public company for five years. The fine amounted to approximately four times what Stewart would have lost if she hadn't acted upon inside information when selling her ImClone stock.[7]

The Savings and Loan Scandal

In the early 1980s, Edwin Gray, head of the Federal Home Loan Bank Board, began to realize that many savings and loans (S&L) banks were in trouble. An S&L bank both holds people's money in savings accounts, paying interest on that money, as well as lending it out to people seeking loans and charging interest. The money in people's savings accounts, plus more that the banks were getting from other corporations, was being invested by the millions in businesses that Gray thought unworthy of the attention.

One of the banks that seemed particularly prone to this activity was the Lincoln S&L, which was funneling money into the American Continental Corporation. The pattern became fishier when Gray discovered that both businesses were run by the same man.

That man was Charles Keating, who just so happened to be a political bigwig, a member of the Republican National Committee. Keating was a regular large contributor to political campaigns. Because of these contributions, Keating might have hoped not to be investigated too closely by any federal agency.

THE PROBLEM SPREADS

Looking at it as the criminal enterprise that it was, Keating was bribing the government to stay out of his business. His business, it appeared, was taking other people's savings and investing them in himself. Keating knew that the best defense is a good offense and

Lincoln Savings and Loan Association owner Charles Keating appears before the House Banking Committee. *Bettmann/Corbis*

used his political clout to lobby the government for changes in the system. Keating fought for deregulation of the savings and loans industry so that the government had fewer rules restricting what he could and couldn't do with money—whether it was his or not. The resulting deregulation was a signal to other S&Ls that they could play this game too, and soon the savings accounts of thousands of people were in jeopardy.

The bribes may have slowed down investigation but they didn't stop it completely. By the mid-1980s the federal government was investigating Lincoln S&L's books. The results determined that the whole corporation was a sophisticated money-laundering system, and the federal accountant recommended that the government seize the corporation immediately. That was not done.

One of the red flags that caused federal investigators to look into Keating's investment practices was his funneling money into the construction of a high-priced hotel in Arizona. Investigators found that the hotel would have to remain three-quarters full while charging $500 per room, per night in order to make money. This was unlikely.[1] Further investigation was warranted. At this time the two-term administration of President Ronald Reagan ended, and he was succeeded by his vice president, George H. W. Bush.

TAXPAYER BAILOUT

Later investigation revealed that Keating had invested at least $100,000 in Bush's presidential campaign. The Lincoln S&L was forced to declare bankruptcy in 1989, which means they publicly admitted that they had run out of money and would not be able to pay back their debts.

Because the government didn't want honest people to lose their savings accounts, tax money was used to "bail out" Lincoln and other S&L's that were out of money. Taxpayers ended up paying billions of dollars because of the S&L scandal.[2] Despite spending millions of dollars to fund the campaigns of many key politicians—veiled attempts at bribery—Keating was arrested in 1990 and his was the longest and most complicated fraud trial in history. He was convicted on December 4, 1991. On April 10, 1992, the 68-year-old man was sentenced to 10 years in prison.

Keating's was just one of many S&L's that went down the same road, pulling the same scam, taking the money of investors and directing it into the accounts of executives.

In the White House the scandal hit very close to home when the president's son, Neil Bush, was investigated for his part in the S&L scandal. Although the money stolen by Keating and the other S&L owners involved more money than all of the bank robberies around the world throughout history, the average prison sentence served by the S&L heads that were convicted was typically one-fifth the prison time that a bank robber would have received.

Chronology

1830 System is put in place whereby Congressmen can write checks beyond their means without penalty, the difference to be paid by taxpayers. The system is not discovered by the public until 1992. The resulting scandal is known as "Rubbergate" because members of Congress could fearlessly bounce checks.[1]

1869 Jay Gould and Jim Fisk unsuccessfully attempt to corner the gold market. Their actions were mostly legal at the time but led to reforms in the law.

1929 The stock market crashes, leading to the Great Depression. The crash was caused in large part by corporate corruption and unchecked greed.

1933 A reporter for *The Nation* wrote, "If you steal $25, you're a thief. If you steal $250,000, you an embezzler. If you steal $2,500,000, you're a financier."[2]

1963 The year of "The Great Salad Oil Swindle," in which the Allied Crude Vegetable Oil Refining Corporation used the simple scientific fact that oil floated atop water to create a great deception.[3]

1963 Billy Sol Estes, a friend of then-Vice President Lyndon Johnson, is charged and convicted of fraud after selling millions of dollars of grain that didn't exist.

1970 The RICO laws are passed, making it easier to arrest and convict white-collar criminals who conspire to commit crimes.

Late 1970s, early 1980s The FBI uses undercover agents to "sting" elected officials in the U.S. government, videotaping the officials as they accept large bribes. This came to be known as the ABSCAM case.[4]

1977 A combination of illegal dumping of toxic waste and a spring melt contaminates the homes of many people in the Love Canal area near Buffalo, New York, and leads to a tragic health epidemic.

1979 A poll in a periodical called *Criminology* showed that white-collar crime accounting for billions of stolen dollars was ranked as less of a problem than street crime involving a theft larger than $25.[5]

The 1980s The "Greed Decade." The number of white-collar crimes skyrockets.

1988–89 The Savings and Loan scandal, the largest white-collar crime ever, drains the savings of millions of Americans and costs taxpayers billions of dollars.

1989 Barry Minkow was arrested, tried, and convicted after inventing a company and then convincing other companies to invest $80 million in it. He served five years in prison.[6]

1995 The FBI arrested computer hacker Kevin Mitnick. He later served five years in prison after pleading guilty to charges of wire and computer fraud.

2004 TV personality Martha Stewart was tried and found guilty in a long and highly publicized trial in New York City. A jury listened to testimony for five weeks and then found Martha Stewart guilty on four counts of obstructing justice by lying to investigators about a well-timed stock sale.

September Andrew Fastow, Enron's formal chief financial officer, and, according to the Associated Press, "one of the key figures in Enron Corporation's collapse," was sentenced to six years in prison.[7]

Autumn After a year-long investigation, the United States Secret Service arrested 28 suspects in eight U.S. states and six foreign countries on charges of identity theft, computer fraud, credit card fraud, and conspiracy.[8]

2001–05 According to the FBI, there was a 300 percent increase in the amount of white-collar crime during this time span.

Endnotes

Introduction

1. "Wex: White-collar crime," Cornell University Law School Web site. http://www.law.cornell.edu/wex. Accessed June 29, 2006.
2. Ibid.
3. "White-collar Crime," Federal Bureau of Investigation Web site. http://www.fbi.gov/whitecollarcrime.htm. Accessed June 29, 2006.

Chapter 1

1. Stephen M. Rosoff, Henry N. Pontell, and Robert Tillman, *Profit Without Honor: White-Collar Crime and the Looting of America* (Upper Saddle River, N.J.: Prentice Hall, 2006), 3.
2. "The National City Bank Scandal," *The Nation* (March 1933): 248.
3. Howard M. Schilit, "Can We Eliminate Fraud and Other Financial Shenanigans?" *USA Today Magazine* (September 1994): 83–84.
4. "Justice Steps In," *Time Magazine* Web site. http://www.time.com. Accessed February 13, 2008.
5. "Futures Regulation Before the Creation of the CFTC," U.S. Commodity Futures Trading Commission Web site. http://

www.cftc.gov. Accessed February 13, 2008.
6. Evan Moore, "Billy Sol Estes: Last One Standing," *Texas Magazine* [insert in the *Houston Chronicle*] (June 23, 1996): 10.
7. "People and Events: Black Friday," PBS Web site. http://www.pbs.org. Accessed February 13, 2008.
8. Rosoff, 7.
9. William Webster, "An Examination of FBI Theory and Methodology Regarding White-Collar Crime Investigations and Prevention," *American Criminal Law Review* 17 (1980): 276.
10. Francis Cullen, "The Seriousness of Crime Revisited," *Criminology* (1982): 83–102.
11. Rosoff, 158-59.
12. James S. Granelli, "Forecast is Now $3.4 Billion to Liquidate Lincoln Savings," *Los Angeles Times* (October 31, 1993): D1.
13. Rosoff, 8.
14. Daniel Akst. *Wonder Boy: Barry Minkow* (New York: Charles Scribner's Sons, 1990), 5.
15. Rosoff, 23.
16. Robert E. Kessler, "Preacher helps find an alleged con man," *Newsday* Web site. http://www.news day.com. Accessed February 11, 2008.

17. Marshall Clinard and Peter Yeager *Corporate Crime* (New York: The Free Press, 1980).
18. Ibid.
19. Phil Kuntz, "Check-Kiting at the House Bank," *Congressional Quarterly Weekly Report* (February 29, 1992): 446–451.
20. Rosoff, 18.

Chapter 2

1. "Antitrust Enforcement and the Consumer," U.S. Department of Justice Web site. http://www.usdoj.gov/atr/public/div_stats/211491.htm. Accessed February 15, 2008.
2. http://www.law.cornell.edu/wex/index.php/White-collar_crime#Federal_Material.
3. Ibid.
4. "Common Fraud Schemes," FBI Web site. http://www.fbi.gov/majcases/fraud/fraudschemes.htm. Accessed February 15, 2008.
5. http://www.law.cornell.edu/wex/index.php/White-collar_crime #Federal_Material.
6. http://www.fbi.gov/publications/strategicplan.
7. http://www.law.cornell.edu.
8. Barry S. Rundquist, "Corrupt Politicians and Their Electoral Support," *American Political Science Review* (1977): 955.

Chapter 3

1. "Protecting Our Financial Institutions," FBI Web site. http://www.fbi.gov. Accessed February 13, 2008.
2. Matthew Daneman, "Roberts introduces degrees in white-collar issues, forensic science," *Rochester Democrat & Chronicle* (September 4, 2006): B1.
3. http://www.fbi.gov/publications/strategicplan.
4. "Crooks and Con Men: The Best Moments and Most Unforgettable Characters," CBS News Web Site. http://www.cbsnews.com. Posted on January 16, 2004.
5. "FBI Information Technology Strategic Plan Synopsis," FBI Web site. http://www.fbi.gov/hq/ocio/documents/itsp.pdf. Accessed February 11, 2008.
6. "FBI Information Technology Strategic Plan Synopsis," FBI Web site. http://www.fbi.gov/hq/ http://www.fbi.gov/hq/ocio/documents/itsp.pdf. Accessed February 11, 2008.
7. "Federal Bureau of Investigation Strategic Plan 2004-2009," FBI Web site. http://www.fbi.gov/publications/strategicplan/stategicplantext.htm. Accessed February 11, 2008.
8. http://www.fbi.gov/publications/strategicplan.
9. "Federal Bureau of Investigation Strategic Plan 2004-2009," FBI Web site. http://www.fbi.gov/www.fbi.gov/publications/strategicplan/stategicplantext.htm. Accessed February 11, 2008.
10. http://www.fbi.gov/publications/strategicplan.
11. "U.S. Money Laundering Threat Assessment," Report of

a working group comprised of representatives from the U.S. Departments of the Treasure, Justice, and Homeland Security, and the United States Postal Service. http://www.treas.gov. Posted on December 2005.

12. "Protecting Our Financial Institutions," FBI Web site. http://www.fbi.gov. Accessed February 13, 2008.

Chapter 4

1. Jim Walsh, "Camden, area experience turmoil, hope," *Courier Post* Web site. http://www.courierpostonline.com. Accessed February 13, 2008.
2. Daneman.
3. Ibid.
4. Robert W. Greene. *The Sting Man: Inside ABSCAM* (New York: E.P. Dutton, 1981).
5. Charles R. Babcock, "Williams Convicted in Abscam," *Washington Post* (May 2, 1981): A1.
6. Rosoff, 287.

Chapter 5

1. Rosoff, 45.
2. "Guides Against Bait Advertising." http://www.ftc.gov/bcp http://www.ftc.gov/bcp/guides/baitads-gd.htm. Accessed February 15, 2008.
3. Patricia H. Holmes, "Con Artists and the Games They Play," press release, Ohio State University Extension, Preble County; and Terri Tallman, Ohio District 5, Area Agency on Aging, 2005.
4. Clinard.

5. James Harvey Young, "The Medical Messiahs: A Social History of Health Quackery in Twentieth-Century America," Quack http://www.Quack-Watch.com. Accessed on April 15, 2007.
6. Ibid.
7. James Traub, "Into the Mouths of Babes," *New York Times Magazine* (July 24, 1988): 18–20, 37–38, 52–53.
8. Deborah Baldwin, "The Cornflake Cartel" *Common Cause Magazine*, (Summer 1993): 32-36.
9. "Three Oil Companies to Pay $63 Million to Four Western States," *Wall Street Journal* (April 23, 1992): A4; and "Exxon Moves to Settle Suits," *New York Times* (January 15, 1992): D4.
10. "Class-Action Status Granted in Airline Price-Fixing Action," *Wall Street Journal* (August 8, 1991): A5.
11. Rosoff, 54.

Chapter 6

1. Eckardt C. Beck, "The Love Canal Tragedy," *EPA Journal* (January 1979). http://www.epa.gov. Accessed February 14, 2008.
2. Beverly Paigen and Lynn R. Goldman, *Health Effects from Hazardous Waste Sites* (Chelsea, Mich.: Lewis, 1987).
3. Rosoff, 83.
4. Lois Gibbs. *Love Canal: My Story* (Albany, N.Y.: State

University of New York Press, 1982).

5. New York State Department of Health Report, August 2, 1978. http://www.health.state.ny.us/ environmental/investigations/ love_canal/lctimbmb.htm. Accessed February 14, 2008.

6. Gibbs.

7. Mitchell Grayson, "Firm Knew of Peril in Love Canal Chemical Waste 20 Years Ago, Investigators Say," *Los Angeles Times* (April 11, 1979): 4, 8.

8. Kevin Johnson, "Firm to Pay $129 Million for Love Canal Cleanup," *USA Today* (December 22, 1995): 1A.

Chapter 7

1. Bradley J. Schlozman, "13 Defendants Indicted in Health Fraud Conspiracy," Federal Bureau of Investigation Web site. http://www.fbi.gov. Posted on July 18, 2006.

2. Office of the U.S. Attorney, Western District of Missouri, "Independence Woman Sentenced For Health Care Fraud," U.S. Department of Justice Web Site. http://www.usdoj.com. Accessed April 13, 2006.

3. Bradley J. Schlozman, "Two More Women Plead Guilty to Health Care Fraud," U.S. Department of Justice Web site. http://www.usdoj.gov. Accessed February 14, 2008.

4. "U.S. Money Laundering Threat Assessment." http://www.treas. gov.

5. Claire M. Fay, "Two Plead Guilty in a Huge International Investment Fraud Case: The Total Amount of the Case Could Exceed $125 Million," Federal Bureau of Investigation Web site. http://www.fbi.gov. Posted on July 19, 2006.

6. Laura L. Frieder and Jonathan L. Zittrain, "Spam Works." http://www.mgmt.purdue.edu. Accessed February 7, 2008.

7. Ibid.

8. "Why Bayesian Filtering is The Most Effective Anti-Spam Technology." http://www.zdnet. co.uk. Accessed February 7, 2008.

9. Greg Wilson, "Stock Crooks Spamming the Globe," *Daily News* (January 29, 2007): 8–9.

10. Ibid.

11. http://www.spamlaws.com. Accessed February 14, 2008.

Chapter 8

1. "Ex-C.F.O. of Enron Sentenced to Six Years," *New York Times* Online. http://www.nytimes. com. Posted on September 26, 2006.

2. Wade Goodwyn, "Enron's Fastow Seeks—and Receives— Leniency," National Public Radio Web site. http://www. npr.org. Accessed February 7, 2008.

3. "Enron botches payments to ex-employees," MSNBC Web site. http://www.msnbc.msn.com. Accessed February 14, 2008.

4. Cathy Booth Thomas, "Guilty of obstruction, Arthur Andersen

becomes the first courtroom casualty of the Enron collapse," *New York Times* Online. http://www.nytimes.com. Posted on June 18, 2002.

Chapter 9

1. "Kevin Mitnick: A convicted hacker debunks some myths," CNN Online. http://www.cnn.com. Posted on October 13, 2005.
2. John Christensen, "Legendary hacker signs plea bargain to win freedom in one year," CNN Online. http://www.cnn.com. Posted on March 18, 1999.
3. John Christensen, "Legendary hacker signs plea bargain to win freedom in one year," CNN Online. http://www.cnn.com. Posted on March 18, 1999.
4. Eric B. Parizo, "Busted: The inside story of 'Operation Firewall'." http://www.Searchsecurity.com. Accessed February 12, 2008.
5. "Nineteen Individuals Indicted in Internet 'Carding' Conspiracy," Press release, Department of Justice, October 28, 2004. http://www.usdoj.gov. Accessed February 7, 2008.
6. "Secret Service Busts Cyber Gangs," *TechWeb Technology News*. http://www.techweb.com. Posted on October 29, 2004.
7. Michael Benson, *The Complete Idiot's Guide to National Security* (New York: Alpha, 2003), 243.

Chapter 10

1. James K. Glassman, "Martha Stewart and Insider Trading," *Capitalism Magazine*. http://www.capmag.com. Posted on February 15, 2004.
2. Jake Ulick, "Martha indicted, resigns: Stewart exits as CEO after pleading not guilty to charges related to her sale of ImClone stock," CNN Online. http://www.cnn.com. Posted on June 4, 2003.
3. Ibid.
4. Ibid.
5. "Stewart convicted on all charges: Jury finds style maven, ex-broker guilty of obstructing justice and lying to investigators," CNN Online. http://www.cnn.com. Posted on March 10, 2004.
6. Constance L. Hays, "Martha Stewart's Sentence," *New York Times* Online. http://www.nytimes.com. Posted on July 17, 2004.
7. "Martha Stewart to pay $195,000," *USA Today* (August 7, 2006): A1.

Chapter 11

1. Michael Waldman, *Who Robbed America?* (New York: Random House, 1990), 92.
2. Ibid.

Chronology

1. Phil Kuntz, "Check-Kiting at the House Bank," *Congressional Quarterly Weekly Report* (February 29, 1992): 446–451.

2. "The National City Bank Scandal," *The Nation* (March 1933): 248.

3. Howard M. Schilit, "Can We Eliminate Fraud and Other Financial Shenanigans?" *USA Today Magazine* (September 1994): 83–84.

4. Robert W. Greene, *The Sting Man: Inside ABSCAM* (New York: E.P. Dutton, 1981).

5. Francis Cullen, "The Seriousness of Crime Revisited," *Criminology* (1982): 83–102.

6. Daniel Akst, *Wonder Boy: Barry Minkow* (New York: Charles Scribner's Sons, 1990), 5.

7. "Ex-C.F.O. of Enron Sentenced to Six Years," *New York Times* Online. http://www.nytimes.com. Posted on September 26, 2006.

8. "Secret Service Busts Cyber Gangs," *TechWeb Technology News.* http://www.techweb.com. Posted on October 29, 2004.

Bibliography

Akst, Daniel. *Wonder Boy: Barry Minkow*. New York: Charles Scribner's Sons, 1990.

Babcock, Charles R. "Williams Convicted in Abscam," *Washington Post* (May 2, 1981): A1.

Baldwin, Deborah. "The Cornflake Cartel," *Common Cause Magazine* (Summer 1993): 32–36.

Christensen, John. "Legendary hacker signs plea bargain to win freedom in one year," CNN Online. http://www.cnn.com. Posted on March 18, 1999.

Clinard, Marshall and Peter Yeager. *Corporate Crime*. New York: The Free Press, 1980.

Cullen, Francis. "The Seriousness of Crime Revisited." *Criminology* 20 (1982): 83-102.

Daneman, Matthew. "Roberts introduces degrees in white-collar issues, forensic science," *Rochester Democrat & Chronicle* (September 4, 2006): B1.

Fay, Claire M., Assistant U.S. Attorney. "Two Plead Guilty in a Huge International Investment Fraud Case: The Total Amount of the Case Could Exceed $125 Million," Official Web Site of the Federal Bureau of Investigation. http://www.fbi.gov. Posted on July 19, 2006.

"GAO: Accountability, Integrity, Reliability," Official Web Site of the Government Accountability Office. http://www.gao.gov. Accessed April 17, 2006.

Glassman, James K. "Martha Stewart and Insider Trading," *Capitalism Magazine*. http://www.capmag.com. Posted on February 15, 2004.

Grayson, Mitchell. "Firm Knew of Peril in Love Canal Chemical Waste 20 Years Ago, Investigators Say," *Los Angeles Times* (April 11, 1979): 4, 8.

Hays, Constance L. "Martha Stewart's Sentence," *New York Times* Online. http://www.nytimes.com. Posted on July 17, 2004.

Johnson, Kevin. "Firm to Pay $129 Million for Love Canal Cleanup," *USA Today* (December 22, 1995): 1A.

"Kevin Mitnick: A convicted hacker debunks some myths," CNN Online. http://www.cnn.com. Posted on October 13, 2005.

Kuntz, Phil. "Check-Kiting at the House Bank," *Congressional Quarterly Weekly Report* (February 29, 1992): 446–451.

"Martha Stewart to pay $195,000," *USA Today* (August 7, 2006): A1.

Moore, Evan. "Billy Sol Estes: Last One Standing," *Texas Magazine* (insert in the *Houston Chronicle*) (June 23, 1996): 10.

Paigen, Beverly and Lynn R. Goldman. *Health Effects from Hazardous Waste Sites.* Chelsea, Mich.: Lewis, 1987.

Podgor, Ellen S. *White-collar Crime in a Nutshell.* St. Paul, Minn.: West Publishing Co., 1993.

Rosoff, Stephen M., Henry N. Pontell, and Robert Tillman. *Profit Without Honor: White-Collar Crime and the Looting of America.* Upper Saddle River, N.J.: Prentice Hall, 1998.

Rundquist, Barry S. "Corrupt Politicians and Their Electoral Support." *American Political Science Review* 71, 3 (1977): 954–963.

"Secret Service Busts Cyber Gangs," *TechWeb Technology News.* http://www.techweb.com. Posted on October 29, 2004.

Schilit, Howard M. "Can We Eliminate Fraud and Other Financial Shenanigans?" *USA Today Magazine* (September 1994): 83–84.

Schlozman, Bradley J., United States Attorney, Western District of Missouri. "13 Defendants Indicted in Health Fraud Conspiracy," Official Web Site of the Federal Bureau of Investigation. http://www.fbi.gov. Posted on July 18, 2006.

Sterngold, James. "Boesky Sentenced to Three Years in Jail in Insider Scandal," *The New York Times* (December 19, 1987): 1, 39.

Thomas, Cathy Booth. "Guilty of obstruction, Arthur Andersen becomes the first courtroom casualty of the Enron collapse," *Time* Online. http://www.time.com. Posted on June 18, 2002.

Traub, James. "Into the Mouths of Babes," *New York Times Magazine* (July 24, 1988): 18–20, 37–38, 52–53.

Ulick, Jake. "Martha indicted, resigns: Stewart exits as CEO after pleading not guilty to charges related to her sale of ImClone stock," CNN Online. http:// www.cnn.com. Posted on June 4, 2003.

"U.S. Money Laundering Threat Assessment," Official Web Site of the U.S. Department of the Treasury, Report of a working group comprised of representatives from the U.S. Departments of the Treasure, Justice, and Homeland Security, and the United States Postal Service. http:// www.treas.gov. Posted in December 2005.

Webster, William. "An Examination of FBI Theory and Methodology Regarding White-Collar Crime Investigations and Prevention," *American Criminal Law Review* 17 (1980): 276.

"Wex: White-collar crime," Cornell University Law School Web site. http://www.law.cornell.edu/wex. Accessed on June 29, 2006.

"White-collar Crime," Official Web site of the Federal Bureau of Investigation. http://www.fbi.gov/whitecollarcrime.htm. Accessed on June 29, 2006.

Wilson, Greg. "Stock Crooks Spamming the Globe." *Daily News* (January 29, 2007): 8–9.

Young, James Harvey. "The Medical Messiahs: A Social History of Health Quackery in Twentieth-Century America," Quack Watch. http://www.QuackWatch.com. Accessed on April 15, 2007.

Further Resources

Books

DeAngelis, Gina, and Austin Sarat. *White-collar Crime*. New York: Chelsea House, 1999.

Gibbs, Lois. *Love Canal: My Story*. Albany, N.Y.: State University of New York Press, 1982.

Greene, Robert W. *The Sting Man: Inside ABSCAM*. New York: E.P. Dutton, 1981.

Kerns, Ann. *Martha Stewart*. Breckenridge, Colo.: Twenty-First Century Books, 2006.

Index

About the Author

Michael Benson is the author of 50 books, including the true-crime books *Betrayal in Blood* and *Lethal Embrace*. He's also written *The Encyclopedia of the JFK Assassination* and *Complete Idiot's Guides to NASA, National Security, The CIA, Submarines*, and *Modern China*. Other works include biographies of Ronald Reagan, Bill Clinton, and William Howard Taft. Originally from Rochester, N.Y., he is a graduate of Hofstra University.

About the Consulting Editor

John L. French is a 31-year veteran of the Baltimore City Police Crime Laboratory. He is currently a crime laboratory supervisor. His responsibilities include responding to crime scenes, overseeing the preservation and collection of evidence, and training crime scene technicians. He has been actively involved in writing the operating procedures and technical manual for his unit and has conducted training in numerous areas of crime scene investigation. In addition to his crime scene work, Mr. French is also a published author, specializing in crime fiction. His short stories have appeared in *Alfred Hitchcock's Mystery Magazine* and numerous anthologies.